M000026874

SURVIVE

THE

DEPRESSION

The Shaking Has Begun

by Andrew Strom

RevivalSchool

THE SHAKING HAS BEGUN

Copyright © 2008 by Andrew Strom. All rights reserved.

Permission is granted to photocopy and pass around copies of this book – so long as it is done for no charge. So yes - you can photocopy it! However, this book may not be reprinted in book form or placed on the Internet without the express permission of the author.

Published by: RevivalSchool
www.revivalschool.com

Wholesale distribution by Lightning Source, Inc.

Scripture taken from the KJV. The New King James Version® is also used on occasion. Copyright © 1982 by Thomas Nelson, Inc. Used by permission. All rights reserved.

ISBN-13: 978-0-9799073-8-8

ISBN-10: 0-9799073-8-1

1. Religion – Social Issues   *2. Economy, Personal Investments*

CONTENTS

CHAPTER ONE

THE SHAKING IS UPON US

For years now, God has been speaking all over the world of a coming crash, a great depression, an economic tsunami. For over a decade our ministry has published these more "generalized" prophecies. But in 2006, while based in America, we began to specifically declare that the U.S Housing Crisis was "it" – and that economic judgment would surely follow. In fact, we began to warn in no uncertain terms that the Housing slump was about to turn into a disastrous Depression.

In November 2007 while preaching in Wisconsin USA, I found myself going even further. I felt a real boldness from the Holy Spirit and for the first time I found myself clearly putting a "date" on this coming Depression - something I had never done before (or even considered doing) - except in the vaguest of terms. I found myself boldly declaring that within six months America would be in Recession, and within 12 months the actual Depression would begin.

(This audio is on our website – http://www.revivalschool.com)

It must have been God, because just ten months later, in September 2008 came the crisis that rocked the globe. The two largest Mortgage giants in the world (Fannie Mae & Freddie Mac) failed, the largest Insurance Company on earth and the largest thrift bank in the USA both collapsed, Lehman Brothers went bankrupt (almost taking the entire financial system with it), Money Markets reeled, the Investment banking industry crumbled, and the stock market suffered its worst-ever one-day loss, plunging 777 points in a single day. As I wrote on our email List during this period, "THE DEPRESSION HAS BEGUN".

WARNINGS UNHEEDED

Just as a bit of background of how we found ourselves in America at the beginning of this Housing crisis, I am a speaker and writer – and back in 1996 while living in New Zealand we had begun a Revival website and Email List that we had no idea would one day take us around the world. (Today these are known as "RevivalSchool.com" and the REVIVAL List). We sensed strongly in the early 2000's that God was calling us to live and minister in the United States for a season, during which time I spoke and warned and ministered right across that vast nation for four years.

But as I wrote on the eve of our departure from the USA at the end of that time:

"I remember just before my first trip to America in 2003, God actually gave me a message while I SLEPT - which had never happened to me before. It was about the "windows of Revival" which open in America roughly every 50 years - and how disastrous it would be if America "missed her next window". When I awoke I went and checked the history books - and there it was! - A 50-year cycle of Awakenings in America - going back 250 years. And they were due for the next one right then! How disastrous it would be if they missed it. And so, on my first trips to America, that is just what I preached. -A very serious and urgent warning that I believe came directly from God Himself.

And now here I am five years later, called by God to leave one of the nations in the world that I have loved the most. We came here longing to see America come into her next Awakening, but now we leave wondering what on earth is going to happen. For years we spent our time urging the people to PRAY, exhorting the preachers to return to a piercing message of holiness and Repentance. My friends, has it all been in vain?...

I fear that a terrible "breaking" must come upon this land before she will listen - for like Israel she has become far too comfortable to even stir herself. I greatly fear that God is about to remove most of this "comfort" - the hard way. And the same applies to much of the Western World - including New Zealand. Complacency and apathy have robbed our affluent nations of their urgency and spiritual hunger. And they are about to pay a terrible price..."

One thing that needs to be emphasized is that I am convinced this 'breaking' is not merely financial in nature. It is also aimed at the church, the media and the culture. As we will see, it involves a toppling of current leadership, a massive shake-up of the way things are done and who heads what – even in the order of NATIONS. We have entered an era of unprecedented change. Many will be demoted and many suddenly promoted by the hand of the Lord.

But to me, the most important changes will take place in the Body of Christ. We are about to see another "Great Reformation" of the church. In fact, it has already begun. It began not long after our family left America, in a sleepy little town called Lakeland, Florida. And within months it was shaking the very foundations of the Charismatic leadership worldwide in ways that had never been seen before. (More on this later).

I believe that there is a strong link between financial calamity and "Great Reformation" of the church. The two go hand in hand. It is clear now that this massive shaking is already upon us. The tidal wave has reached the shore.

A 30-YEAR OLD PROPHECY

One of the most famous prophecies that has ever come out of my homeland New Zealand is called the "Commando Army" prophecy – given way back in December 1977. I believe it applies to more than just New Zealand – and it speaks of exactly what we have just been talking about. It is a very powerful word, which I believe may now be coming true right before our eyes:

THE COMMANDO ARMY

-by Ron McKenzie.

We are nearing a time of great spiritual battle. At present God is preparing a Commando Army which can fight and win under tough conditions with few resources. Then He will drop a bomb which will almost destroy the enemy army and will shatter the conventional forces in God's army.

He will then send in the Commando Army which, because of its training, has been unharmed by the bomb. It will defeat the shattered enemy army. It will treat the injured, and reorganize, re-equip and rejuvenate the shattered forces of God's conventional army. The result will be a mighty victory for God.

The Commando Army is a small group in the church which God is calling into strict discipleship. They will reject the things of the world and live solely on what God provides. Their joy in poverty will be a witness to the world. They will be MIGHTY WARRIORS IN PRAYER. They will experience the POWER OF GOD, being able to minister to all people in all situations. Their sole motivation will be the love of Christ.

When this Army is ready God will drop the bomb on New Zealand. It will be an economic depression on a scale which New Zealand has not seen before. It will make the depression of the 1930's look mild. God will shake the nation. It will have two effects.

Firstly - it will shatter the church. The church has become a peacetime army unaware that an intense battle is raging. The people have been blinded by wealth and have become so satiated that they have sunk into apathy. They have taken a worldly attitude into the church and run it like a business, paying their fees and letting the minister do the work. They have become so worldly that they no longer provide a witness to the world. Under economic depression these people will be totally shattered. They found their security in wealth and now they will have none. They found their happiness in material goods and now they will have none. They run the church with money so it will grind to a halt. It will be a judgment on the church. The world forces will also be shattered. Satan has used the lure of money and material wealth to hold the people outside the church captive and the crash will mean that his hold is broken. Thus, we will have a situation where the church is ready for renewal and the nation is ready for revival.

At this point God will send in His Commando Army. Because its members have learned to live without the things of the world they will not be touched by the depression. They will minister to the church and preach to the nation. The people of the church will be shattered out of their complacency. They will see that their old lives lacked meaning and purpose. They will be looking desperately for something else which is meaningful and fulfilling, and the lifestyle of God's special forces will be an attractive alternative. There will be a great renewal in the church, as people repent and turn back to God. Many will be ministered to and discover a wonderful new life in the Spirit through Christ. Thus God's glory will return to the church.

At the same time the Commando Army will go throughout the nation preaching the gospel. The people will be looking for a new meaning to life and will be ready to receive the gospel. Thus as a result of a great move of the Spirit many people will be added to the church.

The depression will not come for a short while. There are a number of reasons for this:

1. God has only just begun to prepare His Commando Army. They still have a lot of training to do.

2. These events will come when people are not expecting them. At the moment everyone is talking about depression. But things will improve, giving people a new hope, then just when the trouble appears to be past the crash will come.

3. These events will be a judgment on both the church and the nation, and when God judges He always warns first. And before the crash can come, God must warn the church and the nation.

Although these events are a little way away they are inevitable. At present God is calling up His Commando Army, but He is only calling for volunteers. Thus it is a time of decision. If we join it will be costly but it will save much heartbreak later. If we choose to join we must become WARRIORS OF GOD. We must become POWERFUL IN PRAYER. We must learn to MOVE IN THE POWER OF THE SPIRIT, we must lay aside all the things of the world which would encumber us. We must learn to live solely for the LOVE OF GOD. It will be costly, but Oh.. how great is the prize...

A Nation brought back to God..!

[Source: http://www.kingwatch.co.nz – Used by permission].

What a stunning prophecy! I remember getting chills up my spine when I first read it many years ago. I am convinced that God has indeed been preparing an army for this time. Hidden in the silent pews, in the caves and wildernesses, disillusioned with "church as we know it", longing and crying and praying for something more – some of them have been in training for years. Others are the youth who will make up a significant part of God's Commando Army in these last days. What we are looking at is a Great Reformation, a Street Revival, a Youth Revival, and a great Harvest – all rolled into one. And all occurring in the midst of some of the darkest days that the West has ever seen.

Tell me friend, are you ready? Have you been allowing God to train you and break you and mold you for such a time? We live in some of the most momentous days in the history of the church. And only those who are prepared and praying will have a part in what God is about to do. Friend, if you are brutally honest - is that you?

Please notice that there are two main themes to the above prophecy, apart from the "army" itself. One is that a Great Depression is coming, and the other is that this will bring massive shaking and Reformation to the church. AMEN! That is exactly what I believe we are about to see.

FIVE PREDICTIONS OF ECONOMIC JUDGMENT

As stated earlier, it was in 2006 that we first began to publish warnings of the looming Housing Crisis – actually in late August of that year. Below are five words from the years 2006 to 2008 predicting imminent economic collapse in the USA and why it would happen. Such a collapse would impact not just America, but the entire developed world:

(1) "AMERICA IN THE BALANCES" – 14 Dec 2006.
-by Andrew Strom.

Complacency. Apathy. -These are the greatest downfalls of the 'lukewarm' church. "We are increased with goods, and have need of nothing," as the Scripture so rightly says.

So what does God do with a country like America today? -A country that has historically been a "Land of Revivals" but is now addicted to "consumerism" en masse. A country that for the first time since the Great Depression now has a NEGATIVE savings rate - because its people are so enamored with owning "things" - even if they can't afford them. A country whose people are indebted to their eyeballs and beyond - so they can keep up the lifestyle of ease to which they have grown accustomed.

What does God do with an America that has grown too fat to pray?

Is anybody "desperate" any more? Where are those who cry to God from their gut - from the bottom of their heart? Where are the agonies and tears? Has America forgotten what kind of prayer it

- 11 -

takes to obtain an Awakening? If we can't pray like that any more, then surely all is lost?

But just how 'desperate' are things really, you ask? Things aren't so terrible, surely?

Well, the fact is that this nation's sin right now is utterly unmatched in her entire history. Has there ever been a generation of Americans that has killed 40 million babies in just 30 years? No, such a thing is UNPRECEDENTED. And has there ever been an American generation that has not only CELEBRATED homosexuality - but actually helped broadcast and spread it around the earth? No, such a thing has never been seen before. Forty years ago it would have been undreamt-of.

(-God reserves for these particular types of sin the term, "Abominations" - and historically any nation practicing them has been utterly destroyed).

Has there ever been an American generation that has addicted the whole earth to soft porn and violence the way that Hollywood has done in the last 40 years? No, again this is UNPRECEDENTED in history. (The center of the worldwide pornography industry is located just outside Los Angeles).

Has there ever been an American generation whose preachers go on satellite television and teach other leaders in 'Revival' countries how to "milk" the sheep for money, and grow rich at the expense of the poor? No, I tell you, America has NEVER done this before. Our TV preachers are now actually being used by the devil to corrupt true moves of God all over the globe. (Go to Nigeria, Ghana, Brazil and see what I mean. American "Prosperity" is everywhere - and still spreading).

At this very moment America is hanging in the balances. God is making up His mind what to do with her. And yet still complacency rules. -Still no "desperate" prayer. Apathy covers us like a blanket. Will you sleepwalk your way to destruction, America?

Years ago a famous preacher commented that if God did not judge America, then He would have to apologize to Sodom and Gomorrah. I am not sure that it was true then, but I certainly believe it is true now. We are at the crisis point.

In the last 40 years, in every way we have become the most sick, selfish, greedy, corrupt, sin-addicted generation that America has ever produced. And now judgment hangs over the land like a sword.

Where are those who "sigh and cry" at the abominations in the land? Where are those like righteous Lot whose soul was "tortured" day after day by all that he saw and heard? Are there none who will cry to God with strong weeping and tears?

Let me make some predictions at this point, so I can be clear about what this country is facing:

(1) Firstly, I believe it is IMPOSSIBLE to avoid Judgment. This nation may have Revival in the midst of judgments - but this is now the best it can hope for. In fact, without judgments it is doubtful that Revival is even possible. -People are simply too complacent. They need a SHOCK even to begin to pray.

(2) Expect a great economic crash - and expect it SOON. Without this, how will this nation get its eyes off its great god, Money?

(3) Expect further CALAMITY. This nation is "running red lights" one after the other. -That is what 9-11 and Katrina were. Things are going to get much much worse before this is over. Expect something to hit the West Coast - and expect it to be BAD.

It is difficult for me to put into words the crisis we are in at this moment, and the judgments that await this nation if there is no repentance. God is looking for sackcloth and ashes. He is looking for those who "sigh and cry". Will you be one of these, my friend?

The hour is late. The need is urgent. Who will respond?

(2) "HAS THE CRASH BEGUN??" - March 14, 2007
-by Andrew Strom.

In the wake of the Stockmarket turmoil of the last two weeks, I felt it important to comment. Two weeks ago the US stockmarket fell 416 points in one day. Yesterday it lost another 242 points. A lot of this is directly caused by the Housing crash that we have been warning of for the past 8 months or so.

It is only since 9-11 that I have been watching the US economy so closely. I remember very vividly kneeling down by my bed soon after the towers fell on 9-11 and hearing God clearly speak to me- "The HORNS of AMERICAN FINANCIAL POWER HAVE FALLEN." To me this was a profound and shocking word, which I published that same week. I felt strongly that in following years we would see this play out before our eyes. -The unraveling of US financial power in the earth. (I was made to understand it was like the Titanic - which hit the iceberg but did not sink for many hours. In a lot of ways, the sinking of that vessel was symbolic of Britain's decline as a world power from that point on. -I know this is shocking to contemplate regarding the US. -It certainly shocked me at the time).

After 9-11, I continued to publish occasional articles about a coming economic crash. Meanwhile an enormous Housing bubble was building in America.

Eight months ago we began to publish warnings about the bursting of this Housing bubble, and the likely impact it would have - beginning in 2007. ("WORST HOUSING SLUMP in 50 YEARS?" - published Aug 30, 2006).

I began to refer to this coming financial judgment in my sermons, saying that in many ways it would be God's MERCY - to shock us out of our complacency and apathy - and to cause us to desperately seek His face. We have allowed comfort and materialism to turn our heads. We have become lazy - "lovers of pleasures more than lovers of God". Only by striking this country's great idol 'Mammon' can God cause us to cry out to Him. We have no idea how lukewarm we have become...

And now here we are. March 2007. The sub-prime mortgage market is in free-fall. The CDO market is infected. The Yen carry-trade is unwinding. Housing is still sinking with no bottom in sight, and the stockmarket has suddenly become very volatile. It is a slow-motion train-wreck, and this is only the beginning. (-Keep your eye on the DERIVATIVES and the HEDGE FUNDS. -These are the "insurers" of the markets, and systemic danger lurks in their giant shadows).

For some time I have wondered what it will take to get us REALLY PRAYING in this nation. What calamity will need to occur? Do we really need a full-blown crisis staring us in the face before we will go to our knees? -Perhaps we do.

Let me state this very clearly:- This nation is at a crossroads. -RIGHT NOW. What is at stake is an entire lost generation - and in fact, this country's entire future. What will we do? Will we PRAY or will we allow this slide into the abyss to continue?

These few years decide all. -I say it again:- THESE FEW YEARS DECIDE ALL. So what is it going to be?

(3) "STOCK MARKETS SLUMPING - WHY??" - July 27, 2007.
-by Andrew Strom.

Several days ago there was a 200+ point drop in the US Stockmarket. Yesterday there was another 300+ plunge. And today it looks like another rout going on. What is causing this - and does it have anything to do with the "Housing Crash" and other predictions that we have been publishing on this List for the past year or so?

Here is what the experts are saying (-This is from the mainstream Marketwatch website - one of the largest and most respected):

"Around the globe, rout in credit markets accelerates"

"Subprime could create global crisis, economist says"
"World is one "Bear-like' event away from liquidity freeze, Zandi warns"
By Rex Nutting, MarketWatch - Jul 26, 2007.

"WASHINGTON (MarketWatch) -- The problems in the U.S. subprime mortgage market could spiral out of control into a global financial crisis, economist Mark Zandi said Thursday... "Mounting mortgage delinquencies and defaults now pose the most serious threat to the global financial system and economy," Zandi said in his report. "If there is a fault line in the global financial system, it runs through the U.S. housing and mortgage markets," he said. Zandi's comments came as U.S. financial markets reeled from a growing credit crunch..." -[www.marketwatch.com]

As you can see, this "credit crunch" and the accompanying stockmarket declines are directly related to the Housing crisis... Please be aware, this is going to be with us for a LONG TIME. And it is going to get WORSE.

So what do we, as Christians, DO about this?

Well - obviously I am hoping that we have already made moves to GET OUT OF DEBT as much as possible. But the real answer to this question is SPIRITUAL.

I was crying out to God about all this yesterday, and one thing I was strongly led to pray was that this economic crisis will not be "WASTED" on us. In other words, as things grow worse, that this nation will not harden its heart at losing its precious "lifestyle", but rather that its heart will be softened and broken - and become hungry for spiritual things once again. -That the complacency and apathy that comes with materialism will be broken - and people will begin to seek God more and more with all their heart. -That this crisis not be WASTED on us - but that GREAT GOOD might come of it.

For there are two main paths that nations can take when major crises hit - and affect their lifestyle and standard of living. -They can either grow hardened and bitter against God, or they can become more broken and softened and hungry towards Him. We need to pray that the latter will be the case. In fact, we need to be URGENT in prayer that this crisis will not be "wasted" on the Western nations, but that it will prepare our lands for Revival - that it will help to "break up the fallow ground".

As I said, this could go either way, my friends. We really do need to PRAY that our nations will not become hardened, but rather humble and broken and spiritually hungry through what is happening.

All that can be shaken will be shaken. And the harvest fields will be white unto harvest. Are you ready and prepared for this time...?

(4) THE DREADED "D" WORD - Nov 8, 2007
-by Andrew Strom.

People hate it when David Wilkerson talks about it - and they hate it just as much when I talk about it. But right now I have to bring it up again because of what is happening. Yesterday WorldNetDaily published the following:

"Alarm: China signals flight from dollar Investment CEO says he's 'never seen people more nervous'

An unprecedented signal from senior Chinese leaders that the Asian economic giant might abandon the U.S. dollar sent shockwaves through the markets today as the Dow Jones Industrial Average lost 360 points and the greenback fell to a record low against the euro. Xu Jian, a Chinese central bank vice director, told a conference in Beijing, "The dollar is "losing its status as the world currency."" [- Worldnetdaily.com]

A. STROM AGAIN: Actually, according to all the data that I have seen, the Dollar situation is not even the worst of the problems.

There is a global Credit Crunch underway - affecting giant banks and Investment companies the worst - and every day we are getting news of MULTI-BILLION dollar write-downs. All of this is linked to the Housing and Mortgage crisis in America - and its effects are being felt worldwide. -And it is growing worse.

This Credit crisis by itself actually threatens the entire SYSTEM - no exaggeration. And it is already underway - NOW. Many international banks are in crisis mode already - but how long it takes to reach "Main Street" is difficult to know. There is already some fallout. For instance, giant retailers such as Wal-Mart reported yesterday their worst October in over a decade. But this is just the beginning of sorrows.

For many months now we have been saying that this Housing bust will be the worst (by far) that this nation has ever seen. This is no longer a "controversial" viewpoint. Even many of the most mainstream economists now openly admit the same thing.

The "D-WORD" that I mentioned in the title of this article is, of course, the word "DEPRESSION". I continue to stand by my statement of many months ago that within 3 years this nation will be in a terrible financial depression - possibly the worst that it has ever seen. Right now, things are right on track to see this fulfilled.

BUT WHY??

The answer to this question mostly lies in one word - "GREED". There has been an absolute orgy of Greed in this country - from the Investment Bankers selling shady Mortgage-Backed Securities to the condo flippers and Real Estate Appraisers and "Junk Bond" specialists and "Liar's Loan" officers. And what is left is an absolute mountain-pile of shameful, unethical financial garbage - which nobody is willing to swallow any more. -And then there are the DERIVATIVES. -A market worth over $400 TRILLION which, if it ever gets infected by this toxic junk (-which is close to happening), may cause the WORST SYSTEMIC AVALANCHE that the world has ever seen.

GREED is the word. At the end of the day, all of this has been for the love of the Almighty Dollar.

In fact, even CHRISTIAN AMERICANS love the Almighty dollar so much that they are willing to make up ENTIRE DOCTRINES to prove that God loves money just as much as they do. It is a new kind of gospel - never seen in the history of the world before. The Americans invented it and spread it around the earth. And now, even in REVIVAL COUNTRIES, this gospel of greed is taking over. Carter Conlon says that he was in a poor African nation recently where there are 700,000 little children living without parents on the streets - and yet the PASTORS ARE DRIVING BMW's and preaching SELFISH PROSPERITY. Where did they get such sickness? -They got it from America. We beam it to them live by satellite.

And this is why I believe God is about to make an EXAMPLE of the USA. -He has to. All the nations follow her lead. The entire church worldwide looks to her for guidance. And she has become a center of corruption and spiritual sickness almost without precedent in the history of the world. She has made the whole earth "drunk" with her fornications, her movies, her MTV, her music, her rebellion, her love of money. And so I am convinced that God is about to make an 'example' of her before all nations. He cannot have a "Christian" country spreading such things in the earth.

When I am in Nigeria again this February I plan to preach this very thing. -That God is making an example of America so that all the nations will fear. -That this is what happens when you follow a creed of "God wants me rich", of pleasure-seeking, materialism, selfishness and greed. -That God is about to demonstrate to the whole earth what will happen to such a nation. Do you think He is just going to stand by and watch us ruin His Revivals forever?

God has a controversy with you, America. He is girding Himself up for war. I hope you are ready to find out what it is like to get yourself on God's "wrong side".

Enjoy the coming Christmas, America. It may be your last really enjoyable one for a very long time.

(5) HOW TO SURVIVE THE DEPRESSION - Jan 31, 2008.
-by Andrew Strom.

I remember one place that I preached in 2006, predicting that there would be a housing crash followed by an economic depression. There was a man smirking and laughing down the back of the room. I guess that smirk may be missing now.

I want to get into "How to Survive" the coming Depression in a moment, but firstly I need to paint a picture of some of what is ahead. My strong belief is that, particularly in America, this crisis is going to be WORSE than the GREAT DEPRESSION. And it is going to last for YEARS. Other developed nations, such as England, Ireland, Spain, Canada, Germany and even Australasia, are going to be very hard-hit also. China, India and much of Asia will be pounded at first, but I believe will recover faster. All of this is already underway.

How bad is it going to get? I believe that Christians in America need to face the fact that they are about to live through one of the WORST 5 - 7 year periods that this country has ever seen by far. And they need to be preparing NOW. We have not even seen the beginning of the worst of this crisis yet.

I know that there are people on this List who have heavy mortgages - who did not listen to me months ago when I started warning about the Housing crisis. Sadly some of these people are already staring down the barrel of losing everything they own. In fact, millions of American Christians are about to become utterly destitute. A lot of "innocent" and not-so-innocent people are going to get caught out by this. And many ministries that rely on "big money" are going to get crushed.

At the end of the day, this entire thing is a judgment on the great idol of Mammon in this country. God is going to bring that idol down. He is going to smash it to pieces, and separate His true gospel from that of the Mammonites in the church. And woe unto those who get caught under that avalanche when it falls.

Sadly, many poor and underprivileged people in this country are already being affected. We need to have a heart of compassion and be reaching out to these ones as things grow worse.

(By the way, speaking of avalanches, you may remember my warnings about "Derivatives" and the need to watch the "Insurers" of the markets. Already these areas are extremely shaky, and the danger of an "economic tsunami" is high).

HOW TO SURVIVE AND EVEN THRIVE

There is only one type of Christian that I believe will survive – and maybe even thrive – during the coming Depression - and that is the Christian who is ministering actively to the POOR. It does not matter how much gold or US T-bills you store up. It is only "heavenly treasure" that will do. Do not expect to do well if you only selfishly consider yourself and your own family. Those who are ministering to the poor and needy I believe have a chance to literally THRIVE in this situation, while those who "hoard to themselves" can expect God's great displeasure. He is simply not going to put up with it any more.

The other thing that will make all the difference is a strong linking of arms with several others of LIKE MIND. This too is very important. If you are part of a home group, then this may be fairly easy to do. Talk to them about it. Come together in a strong bond of unity between, say, 4 families or individuals. But watch carefully how you choose. These relationships need to be able to survive a prolonged crisis. You may end up LIVING with these people (very likely). And they need to be a good fit ministry-wise also.

These two things - (1) Linking arms with a small close-knit group of Christian believers, and (2) Ministering actively amongst the poor and needy - these two things will make all the difference. And we need to start doing this NOW. Don't wait until the crisis suddenly worsens. That may be too late. Start a "free meal" in your town. Do something! The hour is late.

I believe this is an opportunity for the true Church to come forth and display the Glory of Jesus in this nation - like a beacon set upon a hill. This crisis could be the Church's finest hour - if only we will heed His call. Let the true Church be the one to shine - not the Red Cross, not FEMA. May God's true remnant come forth in this hour to display His compassion and glory to all the earth. It could be the making of the American church – it really could.

Everything I am telling you in this email is so critical, I literally do not know how to stress it enough - it is that vital. There are going to be people who ignore what I am saying here who will literally regret it for the rest of their lives. No joke. You can mark it down.

Some ignored my warnings about the Housing market to their great cost. Others are going to ignore the two things that I am stressing most strongly here - (1) Banding together in small close-knit groups, and (2) Ministering to the poor. And it is going to cost them almost everything.

But this is all I can do - cry aloud and hope that some will listen.

Please pass this on to other Christians who hope to survive the coming crisis, my friends.

God bless you all.

————————————

One of the most important points made above is that this is not just a judgment on the values and lifestyle of the West, but more importantly on the values and lifestyle of the CHURCH. As Ron

McKenzie stated in the Commando Army prophecy: *"The church has become a peacetime army unaware that an intense battle is raging. The people have been blinded by wealth and have become so satiated that they have sunk into apathy. They have taken a worldly attitude into the church and run it like a business, paying their fees and letting the minister do the work. They have become so worldly that they no longer provide a witness to the world."*

The Bible states that "Judgment begins at the house of God", and we need to realize that to the same degree that we have embraced the 'Success Gospel' and 'American churchianity' - to that same degree we ourselves will come under this judgment. God is going to root worldliness and the "love of money" out of His church. He is going to separate the gospel of Ease and Mammon from his pure and undefiled gospel. He is going to drive the money-changers out of His temple. That is what a lot of this "shaking" is all about.

The "gain is godliness" gospel has infiltrated many nations around the globe. The American mega-church syndrome is alive and well even in the Third World – and certainly throughout the West. A lot of it is about money, success, "giving to get", tithing, hype and selfishness. It is the very opposite of "taking up the cross" – the very opposite of "Blessed are the poor in spirit." Basically it is the total opposite of everything Jesus stood for. And He is about to use this crisis to drive it into the sea – along with all who preach it. Jesus wants His church back!

A WORLD-WIDE DEPRESSION

As we have seen, since I wrote the five articles above, the US Housing crisis has morphed into a full-blown Banking and Equities crisis – in fact, a virtual meltdown. And it is set to get a lot worse.

Already a number of nations have been hard-hit – even before this crisis worsened: ie. The UK, Japan, China, and other European nations. And who supplies China, the UK and Japan, etc? Answer: New Zealand, Australia and others. So it has a very serious knock-on effect. There is no doubt that a US-based Depression will cause massive repercussions everywhere.

Not only that, but the housing bust is now occurring worldwide too – with the worst nations (apart from America) being England, Ireland, Spain, Canada, Australia, New Zealand and others. I tell you - this housing depression in these countries is set to last for YEARS. It will be a terrible drag on their economies for a lot longer than most people realize.

I have no doubt in my mind that what we are witnessing is a "changing of the guard" in the economic hierarchy of the globe. Wealth and power are devolving from the West to the East – and this will become ever clearer as the crisis unfolds. This process has actually been prophesied, and I totally believe it. Look for the Asian economies to recover somewhat faster than the USA. And by the end of it all, expect the USA's "sole superpower" status to be in real jeopardy.

It is all very sad. It did not have to be this way. What we are witnessing, tragically, began with a once-great nation turning away from God and His values and His truth. And the price of it all is simply too awful to contemplate.

CHAPTER TWO
RADICAL REFORMATION

I hope after reading the above, that you can see why it makes so much sense that God would use this crisis to purge and cleanse His wayward church. Financial depression and Great Reformation truly do go hand in hand. In fact, this crisis seems almost purpose built to bring colossal shaking and change to the Body of Christ.

The truth is, God is sick and tired of man running the church in his own way – with the arm of the flesh. God wants the reins back! And He is going to take them back whether we like it or not. Below is a very insightful dream that a friend of mine had about this very thing:

RE-TAKING THE SHIP
-by Bryan Hupperts

I dreamed I was aboard a luxury liner, the good ship Christendom, converted curiously enough from a battleship, cruising blissfully through a lazy blue ocean. The cruise ads had promised clear skies, a great time, fun entertainment with some of the greatest speakers and singers of our time, and feast upon feast of a vast array of culinary delicacies from around the globe.

For some odd reason I had the impression this was supposed to be a family cruise but the wealthiest were atop in the luxury suites, quite isolated and protected from the rest of us who were secured in various levels of the ship, each according to our rank of importance and wealth. Somehow, it didn't feel right.

Aside from a growing uneasiness that something wasn't quite right on this vast cruise ship, I was enjoying myself listening to great teachers and wonderful singers all the while surrounded by a few close friends.

One night, as I climbed into my bunk, I felt the ship begin to rock. It was a gentle rocking but soon the ship was tossing and heaving like a fish needing air. People were being thrown out of their bunks and began scrambling to get to the decks. Were we sinking?

I staggered like a drunken man up the stairs to see a sight unthinkable. The deck was rocking violently and everything that could be shaken was being shaken. Baggage and luxuries were being thrown overboard by the cresting of the waves and it seemed the ship would split into timbers. And through the swirling fog I saw what looked like another ship: a pirate ship?

We were being boarded and overtaken. It happened so fast there was almost no resistance. Some from the upper decks were shouting, "You cannot do this. We are the lords of this voyage." And a shrouded figure I took for the Captain of the attacking vessel stepped out of the shadows and replied simply; "It is not to be so among you, for there is only one Lord."

Within a few minutes many of the passengers and crew were in chains for not having "lawfully boarded," while the rest of us were ordered to different decks. The whole ship was in ordered turmoil as everyone aboard was assigned a new place. A man named Mr. Prophet, who had been in irons for most of the voyage for "Speaking Mutiny" against the now deposed former Captain who ironically wore his same chains, was summarily released and placed into the watchtower to be the eyes of the ship.

A woman named Mrs. Intercessor who was serving in the galley as a lowly cook was sent to the deepest hole in the ship. I wondered about her punishment and asked one of the shining soldiers why this was so. He smiled and said, "She is close to the Captain's heart and needs the silence to be alone with him to hear his heart clearly. She has cried out to be released into this 'punishment' for many years. It is a station of great honor."

Others tried to use their former rank to demand an audience with the Captain but he ignored their swagger and boasts seeming instead drawn to the meek and lowly of heart, giving no regard to a person's rank or status.

The ship's powerful self-propelling engines were unbolted and dropped like useless, dead weights into the forgetfulness of the ocean! A mast went up and in a moment, she was transformed from running under her own power back into a sailing ship. Her ancient armory that had been locked tight was opened anew and her weapons were remounted transforming her into both a sailing ship and a warship. Many of the singers quit entertaining and began to offer up worship on the warship. An order was given to the speakers, "Quit merely speaking and teach by example. To your labor stations!"

Some who had beaten their fellow passengers during the voyage were publicly humiliated as a quick trial took place. Those who had abused their fellow passengers were allowed to remain on the ship and surprisingly were treated as guests of the Captain, but even what they had was taken away from them. There was a fast redistribution of wealth and duty as everyone was released into a place that somehow suddenly felt "right." We were no more divided into passengers and crew, but all simply crewmembers, fellow shipmates united under one Captain.

The Captain assembled the whole ship's company and, while holding a bottle of new wine in his hand, spoke quickly. "I come to liberate, not enslave! I have come to reclaim what is mine by birthright. I have retaken this ship that the pirates stole from me. She is no more christened The Christendom, but her true name, the good ship Salvation!"

He broke the bottle of new wine over her bow. "All who will may board her freely for the price to sail has been paid in full. We set sail for my Father's kingdom. Rebels and mutineers, beware! Your day of retribution draws swiftly near. Behold, I come quickly!"

A cheer went up from the crew as the sails were hoisted and a sudden wind from the deepest Heaven began to blow, propelling her towards an unseen land. My last sight was seeing her proper Captain at the wheel with his joyous face yet set like flint for the voyage to come. I sensed troubled waters of tribulation brewing and knew that only with the true Captain at the helm would we safely reach our destination.

[© 2004 Bryan Hupperts – SheepTrax.com – Used by permission].

SO WHAT NEEDS TO CHANGE?

The sad fact is that there is so much that is unbiblical and lukewarm about our Christianity today, that it is hard to know where to start. I once did a study of the early church in the Book of Acts and found that there was basically NOT ONE similarity between the way the original church was set up and ours today. Not one! The things we preach are totally different, our lack of power and authority is totally different, our understanding of "church life" is totally different, our values and lifestyles are totally different, the type of people we focus on are totally different – in fact, just about everything we do is UTTERLY AND COMPLETELY DIFFERENT from the Bible. And in many ways it is the OPPOSITE!

In 1993 God gave me a picture of the church which, if anything, has grown even more relevant today. Here it is below:

A young woman (the Church), clothed in what appear to be white garments, stands in a darkened room. As we draw nearer, we see that her hands are clasped around heavy objects that seem to weigh her down, and she is also using the crook of both her arms to cradle still more heavy objects to herself. Above her, God is reaching down with outstretched hands towards her, but she appears hardly to even notice.

In the distance we see Satan, laughing as he drags at the chains of millions of blinded souls, bound in chains of misery, poverty and sin. Slowly, he is dragging them all towards a huge pit at the far end of the room. Many of them are crying out for someone to free them, to help them.

As we draw nearer to the young woman, we see that the objects clasped in her hands and cradled carefully in her arms are nice homes, cars, appliances, land and possessions. We see also that she has designed her surroundings to make herself as comfortable as possible, with so much food available that she has become obese and fat. The cries of those bound in chains are louder now, and we can see that many of them are suffering terribly from starvation and poverty. Millions of them, including many little children, are right on the point of death. The young woman is too busy watching television to really look at them, but occasionally she flicks them some crumbs off her table. A few of them are helped by this, but millions more are destined to perish without hope in the darkness.

We are getting quite close to the young woman now, and we see that despite her seeming affluence, her white garments have become soiled, tattered and torn. Some of this has been caused by her clinging so tightly to her weighty possessions. We also see that her skin is mottled with a kind of leprosy caused by "secret" sins, lust, untruthfulness, resentment, unforgiveness, etc. The young woman shows no signs of being aware of her condition, and in fact appears totally blind to her wretched state.

Above her, Jesus weeps, crying aloud in anguish. The Bible says that He "loved" this young woman, and "gave Himself for her". Now He is forced to behold her steadily worsening plight. He casts His eyes also over the vast millions chained in misery, sin and despair, knowing that it is only through the young woman that He can reach out and heal them. As we watch, Jesus stretches down His hands yet again towards the young woman, calling for her to reach up to Him so that He can pour forth His cleansing power into her and through her, to wash away her sin and unbelief, and to empower her to reach out to those trapped in bondage and sin. But the young woman's arms are so heavy with houses, worldly pursuits and possessions (which she is unwilling to let go of), that she is unable to reach up to God. And anyway, she is so busy watching television that she can't even hear Him calling to her.

On Sundays, the young woman always goes out. She dresses herself up, and makes her way to a beautiful building where the chairs are all in rows facing the front. The meetings here are known as "church services". The young woman loves to sing the catchy choruses and "worship" God as the superb musicians play. The music is so good that she often can't tell whether it is just the music affecting her or whether she is getting a real "touch from God". Every week she feels "uplifted and blessed", and yet still she remains seemingly oblivious to the agony that she is causing her grieving Savior. While the young woman's life apparently revolves around keeping herself "happy", Jesus, the One who sacrificed everything for her, is left "wounded in the house of His friends."

Often there are men speaking at the "church services" who have degrees and diplomas from Bible College. Many of them give inspiring and entertaining sermons, full of stories, jokes and "illustrations". But none of them ever seem to preach directly on the terrible condition of the young woman. Perhaps they are afraid of "offending somebody".

And so, as God watches in anguish, the young woman (the Church) continues on her worldly way, weighed down with possessions and materialism, tainted with sin, seduced by the cares and pleasures of this world. How long will it be before she comes to Him with a "broken heart and a contrite spirit", crying out for a flood of His mercy and His power to be outpoured upon her? And how long will it be before she throws away her worldly toys and pursuits, to seek His face "with all her heart"?

A REVOLUTION IS REQUIRED!

As we have seen, the church is deeply sick and unbiblical in some absolutely crucial areas. And the world is dying out there! They are dying for lack of Truth and Life from those who should have it the most – the followers and ambassadors of Jesus Christ. We have got to see the Western church turned around! We have got to see Reformation, Restoration and Revival! Whatever it takes, we've got to see a return to real Bible Christianity - even if it means the most gigantic upheaval that the church has ever seen.

We have spoken before about the American mega-church syndrome that has spread around the world. This is more of a "feel" and an 'emphasis' than anything else – and is found even in smaller churches. It combines 'seeker-sensitive' compromise with upbeat music and success principles – to create a whole new brand of Americanized Christianity that is slowly taking over the globe.

Listen to these sad statements about where this type of Christianity is taking us, and see if you can agree:

Despite the thousands in our megachurches today, soaking up the warm entertainment offered to them every week, I want to put it to you that we have lost Christianity. Despite the Christian books now found in our Supermarkets, and the "crossover" of Christian artists into the mainstream, and our Christian mega-stores and CD's and DVD's and Study-Bibles, I want to put it to you that we have lost Christianity.

Despite our lavish Cathedrals in the suburbs (Charismatic or not) with their pastel hues and comfortable pews, their projector screens and $20,000 sound systems, I want to put it to you that we have utterly lost Christianity.

We left it behind somewhere when we shifted our churches from the inner city into the "comfortable" suburbs. We left it behind when we stopped welcoming the addicts off the street into our meetings and started welcoming only the "respectable" people. We left it behind when we stopped preaching "take up your cross" and turned the gospel into a success formula - 'Seven Steps to your Best Life Now.'

Somewhere in our comfortable suburban streetscape with its manicured lawns we lost the real thing. Somehow in our concern for "property values" and a better 'retirement plan' we left it behind. But that is not the worst part of it. The worst part is that we don't know how to get it back again. Or perhaps we don't really WANT to get it back again. The cost simply doesn't bear thinking about, does it? And so, as we drive around in our nice shiny cars with our groovy plastic toys, and attend "church" as we know it twice a week for 2 hours;- As we live a life that is about as unlike Jesus as you can get, a life of comfort and coddling undreamt of by billions around the world;- a lifestyle in the top 10% of the earth today (in debt up to our eyeballs all the while) - the fact is that we don't really CARE that we have lost original Christianity, do we? We are too busy, man. Don't bother us with that kind of talk.

It will all be OK, the preacher tells us. We will all make it to heaven in the end. We are all "decent" people here. We have "prayed the little prayer". We have 'given our heart to the Lord'.

Oh yes. We will all make it, won't we? We are all good suburban church-going folks here.

But what is this? What is that thundering voice I hear? "DEPART FROM ME." 'But LORD... But LORD....'

"I said - 'DEPART FROM ME'. Don't call me Lord. You never truly lived like I was your Lord and you know it. For I was hungry and you gave me no food; I was thirsty and you gave me no drink; I was a stranger and you did not take me in; naked, and you did not clothe me; sick and in prison, and you did not visit me...."

What is the essence of true Christianity that we have lost, my friends? It is simply described by James as follows- "Pure religion and undefiled is this: To visit the fatherless and widows in their affliction, and to keep himself unspotted from the world." (Ja 1:27).

OUR GOSPEL - THE WORST LOSS OF ALL

When I think about the lukewarm state of today's church, and the things that have the greatest impact on our Christianity today, I keep coming back to the fact that we have very largely LOST THE GOSPEL. The truth is, in any era, the gospel that we preach makes all the difference in the world. I have studied Revival history for years, and I want to tell you that the Great Reformation and many of the world's greatest Revivals down the centuries have often been based on this one thing: RECOVERING THE TRUE GOSPEL and preaching it with apostolic anointing and authority. But the fact is that today most of us don't even realize that we have lost it!

Surely there is no tragedy in the world worse than this - the church losing the gospel. We could have a hundred terrorist attacks, or earthquakes, or hurricanes, and it would still not outweigh the tragedy of this one thing - WE HAVE LOST THE GOSPEL. Nothing can compare to this disaster - nothing.

For when you lose the gospel, you lose salvation. People are actually no longer becoming saved. (Remember, Paul said that the gospel is the "POWER OF GOD unto salvation"). And when people are no longer truly becoming saved, you also lose the church. For no true gospel = no true church.

People will tell me that I am being too "drastic". Well, I want to say to you that I am not being drastic enough. In fact, if I were to shout through 1000 megaphones directly into your ears, it would not be possible for me to overemphasize just how disastrous and awful and horrific it is that our backslidden Western church today has - to all intents and purposes - lost its gospel. And in doing so it has lost its very reason for being.

As discussed earlier, we tell everybody that all they need to do is say a little rote prayer accepting Jesus as their "personal savior". Tell me again, does such a thing even come close to existing in Scripture? Can you recall anyone in Acts ever saying, "Just repeat this little prayer after me"? Or "Quietly slip up your hand - no need for anyone to see"?

No, you can't. That is because nobody ever did. It is all a modern fabrication - a complete invention. This is no salvation at all. We act like people can safely forget about CONVICTION of sin and DEEP REPENTANCE and WATER-BAPTISM and getting FILLED with the Holy Spirit. Just "optional extras", eh? But look at Acts and tell me - was there ever such a thing as real Christianity without these things? And what about getting a CLEAN CONSCIENCE (washed in the blood) and keeping it clean? Are we ever told how to walk in that today? To actually "walk" in the washing of the blood of Jesus? To be clean, to be utterly "Clean", to be EVERY WHIT CLEAN?? (The most important thing in the world). Where is this in our gospel? Where is the transformed life? Where is the "freedom" from sin?

We have lost it all. Our people very rarely repent. They often go for years without baptism (meaning, according to Romans 6, that their "old man" is not yet dead - and so they simply cannot live a new life in Christ). Read Romans 6 sometime and ask yourself this question- "If I have not been baptized, then is my old life "buried" with Christ or not? Is my 'old man' dead or not?" This is why the apostles always baptized people IMMEDIATELY.

And then we often fail to get people 'FILLED' with the Spirit right away too - let alone "walking" in the Spirit. Tell me, how are we supposed to have 'HOLINESS' if we have not even been filled with the "HOLY" Spirit? Why do you think that the apostles always made sure that people became Spirit-filled RIGHT AWAY??

Most of us do not even have "Day One" Christianity as it was in the Bible. We have lost the gospel and we don't even know it. We have invented a gospel of 'convenience', a gospel without the cross, a gospel without holiness or the power to live a Christian life. A gospel that shows no-one how to get a clean conscience or how to walk in it. I want to say to you that such a gospel is no gospel at all. And we should be ashamed of ourselves for preaching such a travesty.

No wonder today's church is lukewarm! The gospel is the building block upon which everything else is built. Without it we have nothing - literally nothing. It affects all that we do and all that we are. To lose it is simply the worst disaster imaginable. So how on earth can we get it back?

Well, we have spoken about "Revival" a number of times in this book. And we need to realize that the 'RETURN OF THE GOSPEL' was often the key that brought about these Great Awakenings of the past - the Gospel being restored and preached in power. The longest-lasting Revivals always involved the "return of the Gospel". That is precisely what was happening with the preaching of Wesley, Finney, Whitefield, etc. And it has to happen again today!

So "Revival" to me is far more than just a fleeting visitation. It is to be the long-lasting restoration of the true gospel - and thus the true church also. If we want original Christianity restored today, we must first see the Gospel restored. It is the most important key to it all. Oh God, send such a Revival! Bring back the Gospel and those who will preach it! Those "mighty men and women of valor" – prepared and trained for years for a time such as this. Oh God, don't leave us the way we are!

SO WHAT IS THE GOAL?

The basic answer to this question is that God is desiring a new Reformation to restore full New Testament Christianity to His church. He wants "revived", on-fire, apostolic Christianity back! This is not simply "structural" change that we are talking about here. It involves "heart" change of the most profound kind. People must experience 'personal Revival' and become full New Testament Christians if they are going to gather and function together in a truly New Testament way.

This is a very tall order, but I believe it is exactly what God is wanting to do. And I believe the giant crisis and shaking that is almost upon us is His opportunity to bring it to pass. And He is calling us to co-operate with Him.

A PICTURE OF 'ACTS'-TYPE CHRISTIANITY

To give a positive picture of the kind of Christianity I am talking about, I want you to forget about today's church for a moment - with all her apparent problems and contradictions. Imagine that you are still living in the same city, in the same year, but you are right in the middle of a 'Book of Acts'-type scenario. Somehow everything has changed.

For some reason, all of the Spirit-filled Christians in your city have left their Denominations and divisions behind. They are now committed to the TRUE gospel and true Christianity. And they have begun to fulfill the prayer of Jesus - "That they all may be ONE". They now hold huge gatherings all over the city - right out in the open. And as well as these united gatherings, on most streets there is now a house-meeting, where all the Spirit-filled believers from each street gather together, eating and sharing and having communion, etc. The power of God flowing in these meetings is amazing. Many healings and miracles are happening all over the city.

It seems also that the church buildings and cathedrals have simply been abandoned. No longer do Christians want to hide themselves away behind "four walls". They want to gather out where the people are - presenting Jesus to the whole world. They want to be truly "one body". There is no way that any of their old buildings could contain the crowds, anyhow.

And the men whom God has raised up to lead this vast movement do not seem much like the 'Reverends' or even the 'televangelists' of old. In fact, quite a few of them have never been to Bible College and they seem to be very plain, ordinary people from humble backgrounds. But what an anointing! It is very clear to everyone that these 'apostles and prophets' (as they are known) have spent many years in prayer and brokenness before God - drawing closer and closer to Him. When they speak, the very fear of the Lord seems to come down, and many people repent deeply of their sins. People are coming into a "clean conscience" type of Christianity – and walking in it! Demons are cast out and the blind and crippled are made whole. These kinds of things are happening all the time. The whole city is just in awe of what is going on, and thousands upon thousands are being saved. Even the newspapers and television are full of it.

As soon as someone repents they are immediately baptized in water and hands are laid on them for the infilling of the Holy Spirit. This is expected from day one! And it is also expected that every Christian has a gift and a calling from God - and that they should be encouraged to move forward and fulfill their calling. No longer is there a distinction made between those who are "ministers" and those who are merely 'laity'. Now it is expected that EVERYONE is a minister of the Lord! (However, there are 'elders' – i.e., older Christians to guide things).

Some of the bishops and pastors from several denominations have actually denounced this great move of God very strongly. They say it is "deception" and warn their people to stay away. (Every Revival in history has been accused of this - usually by religious leaders). In fact the persecution is getting worse. But to be honest, it is so obvious to most people that God is the one behind it all, that very few take the opposers seriously. The Spirit of God is sweeping all before Him. The glory of the Lord has come.

One of the reasons that these leaders are so upset is that a lot of the Christians' GIVING now does not go to church buildings, but rather to the POOR. In fact, God has spoken to many people to start supporting widows and orphans overseas, etc. They also feed the poor of their own city and give generously to anyone in their midst who is in need. Some even sell their possessions in order to do this.

The huge overriding theme of this great movement is LOVE. "Behold how they love one another" is the catch-cry of many who watch this 'new church' in action. And everyone is given to MUCH PRAYER.

And so, gathering "as one" in the outdoors (sometimes in arenas if the weather is bad) and breaking bread from house to house, they eat together with glad and sincere hearts, praising God and enjoying the favor of all the people. And the Lord adds to their number daily those who are being saved.

THE REAL THING

The above description is taken straight out of the Book of Acts - as applied to today. Everything in the above paragraphs is put there to give you an idea of what it would be like to live in the Jerusalem church at the start of Acts. And it was like that for YEARS. Imagine the impact of such a church on the world around it! God is wanting to do this again. And He wants to use ordinary people like you and me to help bring it to pass.

I am convinced that we are not supposed to treat the early church as a special case. It was given as an 'example' to us. It is what the "normal" church should be like all the time! And yet we have fallen so far below this standard. Only in times of Revival do we approach it again for a time. But I believe it is supposed to be "normal" for the church to be like this - day in and day out. This is the way that Jesus always wanted us to be.

Even in Spirit-filled circles a lot of traditions are simply taken for granted in the church today that are found nowhere in the Bible. And they are blocking us from coming into the kind of Christianity described above. Preachers may fight to keep them – and probably will. But many of these leaders know deep down that a lot of this stuff is simply the 'traditions of men'. Isn't it true that we have to get rid of a bunch of these things if we are to once again live like the Book of Acts?

I am hoping that this book will make people hungry for a different kind of Christianity - the kind that was actually invented by Jesus and the apostles in the beginning. And I hope that people will understand that it is not just outward 'structural' changes that are needed, but inward 'heart' changes as well. In fact it is the "heart" things that must come first , otherwise nothing of value will ever be accomplished.

So what about you, my friend? Are you willing to do "whatever it takes" to see God restore such a glorious Christianity to the earth? Are you willing to go through tremendous shaking and change in your own life to see such a thing come about? God's eyes are roaming the earth right now for such ones that He can use. I pray that when His eyes alight upon you they will not be disappointed. All that He requires is a willing heart. I pray that you may be one.

CHAPTER THREE
ALL THAT CAN BE SHAKEN

At the very center of the Shaking that is now underway is the Biblical principle – "The kingdom shall be taken from you and given to another." Remember, the prophet Samuel essentially spoke this to king Saul before God stripped him of the leadership of Israel and gave it to David. (1 Sa 15:22-23, 1 Sa 28:17). Jesus also spoke this to the elders and chief priests in His own day – for exactly the same reason: "The kingdom of God shall be taken from you, and given to a nation bringing forth the fruits thereof" (Mt 21:43). Their leadership role was being stripped away because they had been found unworthy – and their place was to be given to others. It was a complete 'changing of the guard' – instigated by God.

This has always been at the heart of every true Reformation. There has to be change at the top – a total revolution in the leadership - for a new era to begin. But notice that king David had to spend years being crushed and broken in the wilderness before he could be trusted to lead Israel. And this is true in our own day also.

For many years now, there have been prophecies all around the world that God is about to visit tremendous "shaking" and a 'changing of the guard' upon His church. We have already seen that today's Christianity is far from ideal - even far from adequate. And today's world is a godless wasteland without hope or meaning for many of our youth. It is at times exactly like these that God has chosen to move in the past. But such moves are often far from "comfortable" for the church. And it is clear that what God has been speaking about is a coming 'REFORMATION', not just a Revival.

As the Bible tells us, Judgment begins "at the house of God" (1 Pe 4:17). He will always set His own house in order before starting on the world. But such Reformations (and their leaders) are often most unwelcome. For they are never "quiet, retiring" men or movements, and everything they stand for often amounts to one giant rebuke for the church. Was Luther welcomed, or Wesley, or Booth? Hardly! In fact, they were some of the most controversial figures of their day. Like Israel with her prophets, the church has rarely greeted Reformers or Revivalists with open arms. In fact, quite the opposite. It has often been the church leaders who have persecuted new moves of God the worst.

I believe that what is coming will bring great shaking and transformation to the entire Western church, not to mention the Christians themselves. For this is exactly the kind of clean-out that is so desperately needed. And God has never shrunk back from sending in His "specialists" and taking such drastic action before, when it has been necessary. What we need is a total Revolution – back to true New Testament Christianity. And the current leaders sadly cannot get us there.

SHAKING BEGINS IN LAKELAND

When a group of the most senior Charismatic leaders in the whole world stood on a stage in Lakeland, Florida in June 2008, I bet they didn't imagine for a moment that they were setting themselves up for the terrible shaking that followed. The man and the movement that they were so publicly endorsing were soon embroiled in the kind of controversy that nightmares are made of. And yet they should have known better – and were pre-warned by many. It didn't take a genius to see that there was much that was deeply wrong in Lakeland. We ourselves published a book against that movement almost the moment it gained the limelight. I am as "Charismatic" as the next man, but blatant error and dubious "anointings" need to be warned-against for the sake of the flock – not endorsed and celebrated by big-name leaders. Yet such is the state of our movement that blindness carried the day – much to the later regret of many.

Do I believe that God "set up" those leaders that day? Yes, I do. For the first time in my life I saw clear evidence that God Himself had taken the field and arrayed Himself against His own leaders. I have never seen this before in all my years, but it was very clear. It does not matter what "spin" they try to put on it. The Lord God has set Himself once more to "put down the lofty from their seats, and to exalt them of low degree". Sadly, it is no longer man that they are fighting – it is God - and all their protests and excuses are in vain. We are about to see a new leadership arise in the church. The old is to be demoted and the new raised up by God. Watch and see. We are in the beginning stages of a Great Reformation. And there is nothing anyone can do to prevent it.

Steven Dobbs from the UK was given a prophetic word in 2005, that "The Church of the USA will be Filtered by Deception":
"I received this from the Holy Spirit in early summer 2005. The Lord showed me that there is going to be a flood of deception infiltrating much of the U.S church in the near future... The Spirit then ministered to me again and showed me that God was sovereign and that this was His will. I saw that although this increase in deception will test the Christians in the U.S.A, it will also filter the global church from the less reliable U.S teaching ministries and reduce their influence in the global body of Christ... I was shown that many were propagating poor, badly emphasized or erroneous teachings. The Lord showed me that He could not allow them to continue influencing the worldwide church as they are at present. This is because we will soon be entering into the end times and this season will test the faith of all of us."

[SOURCE: www.propheciesfortoday.uk.com/listC.php?id=82]

What we are seeing is judgment on the leadership of the Charismatic movement worldwide – a movement that has descended further and further into shallow "thrill-seeking", Prosperity gospels, encounters with strange angels, gold dust, laughing revivals, and every kind of bizarre unscriptural thing that you can imagine. The Lord has had enough. He is taking action to claim His bride back. And such judgments always begin with the leaders first. It is time for the 'Davids' to arise. God will raise up good shepherds to watch over His flock – prepared for years in the wilderness for this time. He is in the process of dethroning the false and taking back His church by force. Watch and see.

(It is also noteworthy that Senator Grassley's official investigation into six of the largest "prosperity" type ministries in America began in November 2007. Again, such a thing is unprecedented in modern times. More shaking).

TESTING & SEPARATION

It has to be significant that many of the parables that Jesus told about the Last Days speak of the people of God being sifted and separated. (For instance, the parables of the "Tares & the Wheat' and the 'Wise & Foolish Virgins', etc). Is it not possible that God might allow deceptions and falsehoods to test His people and begin this sifting process?

The Greek word for 'judgment' used in the Bible often carries the connotation of 'a separating or categorizing'. Thus, in the parables of the Sheep and the Goats and the 'Tares and the Wheat' for instance, we see the people being separated into two distinct groups or "categories" as part of the judgment process. Whether it is "deception" in the last days that will begin this separation in the church (which seems logical), or something else again, one thing is certain: Such a "sifting" of God's people is definitely prophesied in Scripture.

In early 1995, a New Zealand intercessor was given a powerful vision relating to this. (She believed that it was somehow connected with the effects of the 'Toronto' movement at that time). In this vision, she saw the waters being parted, just as Moses parted the sea. The words that she was given to describe what she was seeing were: "TWO CHURCHES". In other words, what she was witnessing was the dividing of today's church into two totally distinct 'churches' or movements. For a time, while the gap between the two sides was still relatively small, Christians were easily able to jump from side to side. However, as the gap widened, this became more and more difficult, and eventually the only way people could get from one side to the other was to jump into the deep rift itself (the sides of which now looked like huge 'cliffs' of water), to be hauled up by people on the other side.

It is significant to note that right down through church history, true and false moves have often brought division and separation amongst God's people. And from the parables that Jesus told, it seems clear that in the Last Days, this 'separation' will be far more final and complete than it has ever been before.

THE INFLUENCE OF AMERICA

We noted earlier that the Scriptural principle - "The kingdom shall be taken from you and given to another" lies at the heart of the process that we now see underway in the earth. There is another Scripture that is also very pertinent: "Many that are first shall be last, and many that are last shall be first." (Mt 19:30). This applies not just to individuals but right now even to nations and Continents. We have entered a time of great upheaval, when the very destiny of entire regions and lands is in flux. Many that have been prominent and affluent "leader nations" are about to be brought low, and many that have been poor and obscure will be raised up to prominence. "The first shall be last and the last, first."

Now, in what I am about to say, please do not think that I am "anti-American" or any such thing. I lived in the USA for four years and have many wonderful friends in that nation. In many ways it is a land that I love. However, we can no longer deny what American media, television, books, preaching, music or films are doing in the earth. In many ways they are helping to utterly destroy righteousness and truth around the globe.

We saw in the 2005 prophecy quoted above that God is moving to "filter" or limit the influence of American Christianity worldwide.

And it certainly seems that this is the case. I believe that we are about to see precisely the same thing with American influence generally. (I say this with great sadness).

A lot of people don't seem to realize just how utterly dominant America has been in the areas of entertainment, culture, propaganda, media - and the "values" from these things that pervade the whole earth. In fact, America is far stronger in these areas than she is in military might. Her influence pervades every corner of the planet - her TV shows, her movies, her music, her fashions, her satellite broadcasts. Quite simply, America is the "propaganda center" of the earth. And the youth of the entire planet increasingly get their values and their worldview from these things.

If you go to Poland or Hong Kong, Ireland or New Zealand, Israel or Japan - right around the globe you will find American culture everywhere - and usually it is totally dominant. The values of an entire generation are being molded by this media deluge. When I was growing up in New Zealand in the 1970's it was mostly "harmless" stuff like the Brady Bunch or the Waltons. But look at what America is broadcasting to the world now: Sex & the City, Big Brother, 2 ½ Men, Desperate Housewives, Paris Hilton, Queer Eye for the Straight Guy, etc. Television for teenagers has simply never been as sick or sin-soaked as it is now. Not to mention that every music video is utterly filled with explicit sexual themes and violence. America, what are you doing to the youth of the earth?

Let me ask you a simple question: What is the major force promoting homosexuality on this planet today? Answer: It is American television, movies and music. How do they do it? By filling TV shows with subtle propaganda; by making movies like "Brokeback Mountain" and then awarding it with three Academy Awards and sending it around the globe; and by promoting huge 'Gay Pride' events, etc. (Gay marches have now spread worldwide - largely from America). Can anyone tell me what God does to civilizations that celebrate and promote homosexuality in this way? -And use their influence to spread it as far as they can?

How is it that with the godly history she has, America has become the center for the promotion of homosexuality, promiscuity, teenage sex, drugs, materialism, relativism and every other sickness, right around the whole earth? How is it that she has become the great corruptor of the youth of the entire planet? How is it that a "Christian" country has basically become the "propaganda arm" of the devil? Why is it that the center of the pornography industry, and almost every other sick thing, is based on American soil? And what can we expect God to do about this, and how soon can we expect Him to do it?

The amazing thing is, almost all of this has taken place within one generation. Fifty years ago, most of it would have been totally unheard-of. Tell me, has there ever been any other generation of Americans that killed their unwanted babies or celebrated homosexuality and fornication and depravity to the degree that is happening now? Can we go back in history and find any generation that even comes close to being as sin-soaked as this one? And can we find a generation of Americans that spread these things over the whole planet - and made huge financial profits by selling corruption to the youth of the earth? No - we cannot find such things. Nothing even comes close. This generation is unique in American history. We really have to look in the Bible to find anything like it - in the days of Sodom and Gomorrah. Seriously. The USA has never seen anything like this before. And God cannot continue to have it so.

It is not just the secular media, either. As mentioned earlier, Christian TV from America is having a terrible corrupting effect in many Third World nations around the globe. Basically, there have been huge Revivals taking place in Asia, Africa, and South America in recent years - but sadly as these Revivals occur, American influences start to enter in, and before you know it, full-blown "Prosperity" doctrines have become the order of the day. The US television preachers that are beamed in via satellite are particularly harmful. Their obsession with MONEY, hype, flashy suits, and their "success, health & wealth" gospel - all these are having a terrible effect. In essence, what is happening is that God is bringing Revival, and then these televangelists are corrupting and ruining these precious moves of God with their doctrines. Can you imagine "Prosperity" being preached to poverty-stricken peasants? Can you imagine Third World pastors who live like kings? All this and more is what is taking place all over the world. And again, sadly, the center of all this corruption is America. She is broadcasting sickness to the whole earth.

It is very difficult for me to stress strongly enough the grave danger in all of this. Do we not realize that entire cities and empires have been destroyed for the very things that America is spreading around the globe? Do you think God takes it lightly when one particular nation ruins His Revivals and corrupts the youth of the whole planet?

I believe we are about to see American media influence greatly curtailed in the earth. It will diminish and shrink. And gradually, as I stated in the first chapter, I believe we will see overall American prominence shrink also – even her military might. This is all very tragic and sad, but the judgment of God is upon the leaders in the earth – and America is a leader. She has become a poor shepherd and she needs to be replaced. In fact, the entire Western world faces the same fate. The West is corrupt, materialistic and sick - while genuine Christian influence is increasing massively in places like Africa, South America and China. As the economic crisis bites – plus other calamities – expect Western influence to decline and power to shift eastward. "The kingdom shall be taken from you and given to another." Sadly it is already underway. Watch for it.

A TIDAL WAVE OF CHANGE

One of the most powerful visions that I have ever come across related to all this was given to a Christian lawyer from India named Swarna Jha – a woman who has received many stunning visions and prophecies. This one was given to her in August 2006:

VISION: JUST ONE ROAR OF THE LION
-Swarna Jha.

I saw this vision on the 22nd of August 2006.

I saw a Lion. I walked with Him to a very high Rock. The Lion then climbed the Rock, and Stood on the very top of this high Rock. I stood below, looking up at Him.

He let out a LOUD ROAR.

And EVERYTHING in the atmosphere / universe changed.

In a flash I had a 360 degree vision, and what I am about to relate happened in a flash, but I spent the whole of the 22nd of August, just waiting on God, to see in 'slow motion', what I had seen in a speedy flash, and understand what I had seen.

I was told that my mind could not grasp the vastness of the changes I saw in the Vision. So I stayed at home, and did not take up any duties but spent the whole day, off and on, every few hours just re-visiting this vision and seeing it unfurl in more detail, now at a speed that I could cope with. I don't think I have ever seen such a lengthy vision, condensed into a 360-degree vision flash before.

Frame by frame this is what I saw:

I saw Empires fall, and wars begin.

I saw that where previously, formulas and general understanding were proven, it did not work any more, where there were people and places overflowing with money one moment, the next morning the moneyed had nothing.

I saw many 'proven' thoughts, and ways now nullified.

I saw that the balance was tipped in favor of the East.

I saw Angels who had been working in the North and Northwest, recalled and sent East.

I saw children snatched out of the hands of some of the parents.

Fresh food stopped in the western area and was diverted to the East. The fertile became barren and the barren became fertile.

All this, from Just One Roar of the Lion.

I saw 3 long lines of writing in the sky. It read:
Lost, Lost, Lost.

But below it I saw the word:
Gain , gain, gain.........where this line ended I could not see, as it just continued on, endlessly.

I saw that the East gained money, food, etc.

The losses were loss of power, prestige, money, position.

I saw:

Where a soldier stood to load his gun, to shoot, even the last single bullet he had was taken away.

Where a soldier stood ready for packing his gun, where truce had been declared, divine bullets loaded his gun, and led him to shoot.

In the Universe, expected cosmic events were diverted and unexpected ones were brought forth.

Deserts bloomed, greenery was made barren. Light that had focused on the West, now moved East.

This was so sudden that it was like saying..."One morning I woke up, and all was changed".

(Scripture: Amos 3: 8:)
"The lion hath roared, who will not fear? The Lord God hath spoken, who can but prophecy?"

The Lion has Roared.

Dark clouds disintegrated from one place and gathered in another. Whilst there was a West to East exchange on a large level, on individual levels there were changes too. Everything, everything, everything, was changing.

All this from Just One Roar of the Lion.

Just that One Roar, and things from here, were flying there and vice versa. People/ Nations, who had got used to a way of life/of thinking, were in for either a shock or a surprise.

CHANGE, CHANGE, CHANGE, CHANGE, CHANGE, CHANGE, CHANGE.

The hungry were fed, and the fed, went hungry. All opposites were happening. Many homeless were housed, and many of those with homes, became homeless. Light became dark and dark became light. Whatever the present situation, the opposite was happening.

Many rich became poor and many of the poor became rich.

All this, from Just One Roar of the Lion.

Clouds that were meaning to rain, suddenly disintegrated and it rained elsewhere, where least expected.

People were in puzzlement. They said to themselves, "But I thought...." No nothing would be as "I thought."

Many were saying, "But it always worked this way". Now no more. For those who said, "It's never worked for me," they were surprised to know that it will, now.

Heralds blew trumpets, proclaiming: "End of empire, end of empire".

Anyone who had been a Specialist, Monopolist, the kingpin in any area of his life/business, now that would begin to end. Nations that had empires or aspirations building towards it, would now see the beginning of the end of those empires.

Nothing was the same. Everything, everything had changed.

Just One Roar Of The Lion.

And He Has Roared.

Empty pockets were filled, the filled emptied.

Strategic changes were taking place. Whatever had worked like clockwork, would not work now. People of peace were making war, and warring nations calmed down.

For the warring nations it was like the wind was taken out of their sails.

Just as Egypt, Persia, Babylon, Rome, Britain, etc, were all once super powers/empires, but their reign and era ended, so now any 'super power'/ or aspirations thereof, was being diffused. Nations that were looked up to were now beginning to be looked down upon and vice versa.

Balance of power and favor had shifted East.

Angels in the West, held Gold Books. One book was titled "Most Wanted", the other, "Most Favored".

'The Most Wanted' Book had living photographs of the most evil people, the traitors etc. Each one was dealt with and disposed.

The Most Favored, in the other gold Book with living photographs, were some of those, who had lived through most desolate conditions, such were lifted up.

(All that is related here, remember was happening all at once.)

In the midst of all this, I heard the Angels sing: Glory, Glory, Glory.

Time was speeded up in some places, in others, it was slowed down. Wild beasts were all crouching in fear, afraid. I saw the milk inside of cows, curdle.

Just One Roar Of the Lion.

I saw Angels collect gold crowns from those in the North, and they dipped the crowns in a smoky place (the kind of smoke one sees with dry ice), when the crowns emerged from the smoke, they looked exactly the same, but now they were silver.

No matter in which direction I looked all had changed.

It seemed that the very nature of nature changed.

Volcanoes that were dormant, the ashes were removed, and a new fire was lit in them. It seemed that certain species suddenly became extinct.

Reams of paper fell from the sky; paper and pens were sent down, for Chroniclers and Historians, for it was going to be a busy time for them.

Nothing of all creation was left untouched, at Just One Roar of The Lion.

Outside, the earth looked still, but within were rapid-fire changes. Quick, sudden, some were devastating, others surprisingly favorable, but this favor was mostly for the East.

I saw what looked like a flight-path that normally airlines describe on their brochures, as routes of flights/destinations.

For prophets, their flight -paths were moved from here to there, as if randomly, but it was not random, it was the Plan of God for prophets. Prophets will be suddenly moved, and see things from a new vantage point.

I saw some people become tar, whilst others became fountains of water.

Just One Roar Of The Lion.

Many changes took place in the Universe.
On earth, snows of old melted, and water in unlikely places froze.

It is no ordinary thing, when the Lion Roars.

Those dressed warm in the winter, had their clothes taken away, they were left naked. But the naked street-dweller was clothed. There was a divine transfer of wealth, knowledge, and understanding.

People, who'd talked and talked for years, had their mouths taped. But as in Ezekiel 24: 27, those that had been mute for a season, now spoke.

As the vision progressed, I heard the Lord Say: "My People have no roof over their head. I Am their Roof."

I was flown speedily, over building after building, and as we flew, I heard the Lord Say: "Not Mine, not Mine, not Mine, not Mine, not Mine, not Mine, not Mine."

Now I was despairing. What then was God's?

Then I was shown, people in the fields, with instruments. They had no roof over their heads. These were God's own.

The buildings we flew over, were demolished by an elephant's trunk and many T.V. Studios had a fire underneath them. Apparently these buildings had been re-built on the same grounds where prior buildings had been condemned and burnt. These new buildings had been built on the foundations of charred remains, and ashes.

All that was up to the present became obsolete, and new technology, the secrets of which were hidden in nature, appeared.

Science made simple but profound discoveries. I saw Scientists have a 'Eureka' moment. For many who were researching, studying, looking for, the 'thing', it was right there before their very noses. Once they saw it they slapped their foreheads, lamenting, "Silly me!"

Follies of science were exposed. The simplicity of the discoveries to come, were mind-boggling.

Just One Roar Of The Lion.

The very nature of nature seemed to be changing. It was as unbelievable as Isaiah 11: 6-8, 'The wolf also shall dwell with the lamb, and the leopard shall lie down with the kid..."

In some places, I saw an overabundance of wheat, which flowed into the sea, as it was so plentiful. But in other places, I saw land, which was once green, and was now parched land, where nothing grew. I saw beautiful blooms on cactus/desert plants.

He, who understands these changes, will prepare.

The Earth was in a global eclipse. One half had light, the other half was in darkness. It seemed that plates were shifted/ removed from the earth. There were people who raged against God. "We'll do what we have to, let Him do what He wants to", they were saying.

Trees trembled. They knew that their time to be cut had come. To many, prophets and counselors were restored, but from others, the prophets and counselors departed. Sadly from those they departed, noticed it not.

Focus/emphasis of the Church, and the world, due to the presence of new circumstances, changed.

All this, by Just One Roar Of The Lion.

[SOURCE - http://visionsoftheseer.blogspot.com. Used by permission]

CHAPTER FOUR
SAULS, JONATHANS & DAVIDS

There may be some readers who think that in discussing this massive Reformation of the church I have been guilty of inciting 'rebellion against authority'. This is far from the truth. In fact, as this chapter will show, I am very keen to uphold all God-appointed authority. However, due to the seriousness of today's situation and the strong warnings that God has been giving right around the world, I would have been very remiss not to strongly warn of what God has been saying. I only wish that things were different, and that I did not have to say many of the things that I do.

No Revivalist that I have ever read about was a "popularity"-oriented, or 'man-pleasing' type of leader. (In fact, usually quite the opposite!) These were certainly not men to be trifled with. They knew when to be gentle, but were also never afraid to "reprove, rebuke and exhort" with all Godly authority where necessary. They were strong yet balanced leaders - firm but fair. Their love for God and for the people (in that order) enabled them to make allowances for people's frailties, but also meant that they never gave the devil an inch. Such anointed leaders as these are sorely needed in our day, and there can be no doubt that this is exactly the kind of leadership that is about to arise in the coming Reformation. (For God must have His 'mighty men of valor' as always - His Joshuas, Elijahs, Gideons, Pauls, Luthers, Wesleys, etc, to lead His people on to victory, just as the devil has his 'heroes' also).

However, while we may know and look forward to many of these aspects of the coming move of God, the fact is that most of us are still having to deal with the "old" set-up, the church system as it exists today. And no doubt many of us have struggled with exactly how we are to approach our relationship with this current set-up. What should our attitudes be towards today's leaders, for instance, in situations in which we are personally involved? How would God have us relate to these leaders? And how can we recognize the seeds of 'rebellion' in our hearts? These are very important questions, and they are some of the major points that we will be discussing in this chapter.

In working through these issues in my own life, God has very clearly pointed me to the well-known "rebellion" lesson contained in the story of king David. What I want to do in this chapter is to take a fresh look at the story of David, Saul and Jonathan, from a slightly new perspective. One of the main focuses, of course, will be the tremendous godly attitudes that this man David had.

You will no doubt recall how that King Saul had fallen into compromise, presumption and rebellion, and that the prophet Samuel had told Saul that the kingdom would be taken from him and given to another. The prophet then went and anointed David to be the future king. However, there was to be a time of waiting and preparation before David could assume the leadership of Israel. It is my belief that this equates directly to the current situation. I believe that there is definitely a "David company" of future 'leaders of Israel' (ie. the Church) whom God has been preparing in secret for many years right around the world. (These will be the apostles and prophets, etc, of the new move of God). Most of those who are part of this "David company" will already know who they are. Many of them will have received their first or even their second anointing (remembering that David was anointed THREE TIMES before he became leader of all Israel), and will probably already be operating in their calling to some degree.

One thing is certain: This will be a company of PROPHETIC PEOPLE - people whom God has been speaking to about the 'things to come'. Such people will often have great difficulty fitting into the present system, for essentially they will have been "designed" for tomorrow's church, rather than today's. They will often feel like misfits, and may be misunderstood, persecuted and maltreated by those who identify themselves strongly with the present order. Often the powers-that-be will see them as some kind of "threat".

Such was the case with David. For years Saul's jealousy and rage caused him to have to flee for his life. Pursued relentlessly by Saul and his men, David was forced to hide out in caves, in the desert, and for a time even amongst the Philistines! How hurt and lonely he must have felt at times! Here he was, the one whom Samuel had anointed to be the future king of Israel, now an outcast, persecuted, maltreated, slandered... And this went on for years.

But now we come to the part of the story that applies directly to the major theme of this chapter. Remember, Saul was still king over Israel, even though he had already been rejected by God. He was still positioned as the leader of God's people. Now here is the crucial question: What was David's attitude toward Saul all this time? The answer is very simple: David was utterly constant in his genuine respect and honor toward him. He would make no move to try and wrest the leadership away from Saul (as he could have done). He was very aware of God's timing, and he would make no move to circumvent it. Twice he could easily have killed Saul and the kingdom would have been his, but he chose instead to demonstrate real honor and love toward him. When news reached David that Saul was dead, he wept and mourned over him. He had still held out hope for Saul, and had treated him as the rightful leader of God's people, right up until the day that Saul died.

It is my belief that by-and-large, there are essentially three types of leaders or ministries operating in today's Christian world: the Sauls, the Jonathans and the Davids. Let us look at each of these in a little more detail (and I warn you, I will be very 'frank' in this):

1. THE SAULS. These are the Christian leaders who have firmly aligned themselves with the present order, with its compromise, its soulish love of experiences, it's rejection of seeking true holiness, it's love of "pleasures" more than love of God, etc. Sadly, such leaders will often welcome any new Christian fad, so long as it doesn't cost them too much, and so long as it helps keep the people involved in the church. (This is why they have often welcomed new 'church growth' models and methods, etc). Beyond this, however, they stand firmly for the status quo. The thought of TRUE Reformation would absolutely horrify most of them (which

is why they will oppose or persecute any genuine 'Davids' that they can identify). And when the new David-type ministries arise in their church, they will often attempt to "stomp" on them, to dominate them, or if that doesn't work, to limit their influence as much as possible.

To the Sauls of today's church I believe God would have me say: Because you have made yourselves "lords" over the church in Jesus' stead, God will snatch the royal scepter from your hands. And because of the compromise that has been found in your mouths for so long, God will lay much of the blame for the sickly state of today's "lukewarm" church directly at your feet. You have been rejected by God as being unfit to lead His people. "The kingdom shall be taken from you and given unto another" (See Mt 21:43, 1 Sa 15:22-23, 1 Sa 28:17, etc). "Behold, you despisers, and wonder, and perish: for I work a work in your days, a work which you shall in no way believe, though a man declare it unto you" (Acts 13:41).

It is interesting to note that the most serious sin that Saul committed in God's eyes (the sin that finally caused him to be rejected by God as unfit to lead His people) was that after the battle with the Amelikites, Saul compromised what God had said by allowing his men to take the best of the enemy flocks as spoil, instead of killing them all. This 'men-pleasing', rebellious disregard for God's word, caused Saul to be immediately told that his kingdom would be taken from him and given to someone else. "For rebellion is as the sin of witchcraft, and stubbornness is as iniquity and idolatry. Because you have rejected the word of the Lord, He has also rejected you from being king" (1 Sa 15:23). Notice that it was not Saul's 'control' or domination of the people that caused him to be rejected by God, but rather his WEAKNESS AND COMPROMISE as a leader (ie. his desire to be pleasing and accommodating toward his people at the expense of God's word). Is it not the same today also?

2. THE JONATHANS. You will no doubt remember how that Jonathan, who was Saul's son, had a tremendous devotion and love for David. They were like brothers. While Saul went about trying

to kill David, Jonathan was doing his best to quietly protect and help him. I believe that there are quite a number of leaders and ministries around the world today who are just like Jonathan. They have definitely been "friends of the true Revival", But like Jonathan they are caught between their allegiance to the 'old' or existing order, and their affinity with the new ministries - the "Davids". They want to be part of the great Reformation that God is about to send, but they are just too attached to the old system and the old ways to really let go. (Compromise again!) This is a very dangerous position to be in - in a very real way, just as dangerous as that of Saul. For it is very significant that even though Jonathan was a friend of David (ie. a friend of the "new move of God"), he was KILLED ON THE SAME BATTLEFIELD and on the SAME DAY THAT SAUL WAS KILLED. Jonathan never got to see or enter into the new move of God at all (ie. the reign of David). In essence, HE SUFFERED EXACTLY THE SAME FATE AS SAUL.

Another thing that is significant about Jonathan was that he was the "heir apparent" (ie. the 'obvious' choice to lead Israel in the new era, when Saul was gone). I believe that many of today's "Jonathans" are also like this. They are the seemingly 'obvious' Revival-oriented leaders of today - the kind of men who preach on Revival, prophecy and prayer, etc, but in an "acceptable" kind of way. Many of them are truly prophetic, but they fit into the current set-up just a little too well. They have a 'reputation' to uphold in the existing system, and they can be trusted not to say anything too "radical", or to rock today's "Laodicean" boat too hard. They are certainly nothing like the stench in Saul's nostrils that David was. No-one feels particularly 'threatened' by their presence.

As I have said, I believe that there are quite a number of Jonathans in ministry all over the world today. The greatest danger for them is that because of their current respectability and their attachment to the existing order, they just can't imagine God bringing judgment upon the very systems and 'streams' that they have formed relationships with. They love David and all that he stands for, but they just cannot let go of Saul. Deep in their heart they are still clinging to a kind of "acceptable" amalgam between both the existing order and also the new move of God. (It will never happen).

Today's Jonathans would be quite happy if the 'new wine' could somehow be crammed into the old wineskins. They have their feet in both camps. And the terrible likelihood is that when the day of decision dawns, when that fateful hour arrives, because of their double-mindedness they will surely be found with Saul, rather than with David. And this can only result in tragedy. Their failure to see the signs that it is time to finally abandon Saul, and throw in their lot entirely with David, means that they will surely be caught up in the very judgment that falls upon Saul. Sadly, all the signs are there that the cry, "How have the mighty fallen" is about to ring out again in our day.

3. THE DAVIDS. As we have seen, by and large, the reign of king Saul was not a particularly happy time for David. However, I believe that this long, enforced period of brokenness and humility in David's life was ABSOLUTELY ESSENTIAL in preparing him to become a truly Godly leader of Israel. It was at this time that David could easily have become a 'rebel', deliberately stirring up dissension against Saul in retaliation for the way he was being treated. Remember, David had already been anointed by Samuel as the future leader of Israel. He was a renowned warrior, a natural leader, a mighty man of valor. If he had wanted to, he and his men could have stirred up a great deal of trouble for Saul. But instead, with great patience and forbearance, David endured all things, respecting Saul's authority, not murmuring or causing dissension against him, etc. And I truly believe that as much as possible we are to be like David in our attitude towards the church leaders in our own situations today.

Even though there must have been times when David felt extremely distressed, angry and hurt at Saul's treatment of him, he never allowed this to become a festering wound of resentment that would cause him to "react" in rebellion against Saul. I truly believe that if David had acted out of rebellion, then he may well have proved himself to be unworthy of his calling to lead God's people.

I do not believe that God ever sanctions rebellion. In fact, as we have seen, it was because of REBELLION that Saul had been rejected as king in the first place. I believe that God was watching David to make sure that this kind of rebellion was not found in him also. And of course, He is watching us for the self-same reason.

I am convinced that God would have even the Sauls amongst today's Christian leaders treated with genuine respect and honor, right up until God Himself acts to strip their authority, and to anoint and raise up the Davids in their place. (Please note: It is GOD who will do this, in His own perfect time). Until that time, I believe that we are to willingly give today's leaders genuine honor and loyalty as befitting God's appointed leaders over His people. We are also to GENUINELY LOVE THEM AND PRAY FOR THEM. Remember, David mourned and wept over Saul when he died. What depths of Godliness this man David had! And I firmly believe that God is calling the Davids of today to be of this same spirit. We are certainly not to be like Absolem, who sat in the gates of the city some years later, murmuring and subtly turning the people to rebellion against king David. Rebellion is sin, and every one of us needs to ask God to search our hearts to see if there be any "wicked way", any dark seed of rebellion, found in us.

In saying all of this, I do not want people to think that I am advocating some kind of abject, unthinking "slave-submission" to leaders (where you don't "think" - you just do what you are told). This is certainly not the kind of relationship that David had with Saul. In fact, while David was utterly constant in his genuine honor and respect for Saul, he also did his best to avoid him as much as possible, even when Saul assured him that he would be safe! David and Saul were of opposing spirits, and "how can two walk together unless they be agreed?" They were by no means real 'friends' or natural allies. This is the way it has always been between these two opposite types of leaders. One walks under God's special favor, and the other (who once knew this divine favor himself) now does not, and in their heart of hearts they both know it. (Which is why the Sauls are so jealous).

It is also important to note that after Saul had 'died' (ie. had his authority and anointing finally stripped by God), David was appointed as king of Judah (ie. as the anointed and recognized leader of his own tribe). After being anointed to lead Judah, David now had no hesitation in waging war on the "house of Saul" for the leadership of the entire nation of Israel. This was no longer rebellion. David was now the only rightful, God-appointed leader of the whole kingdom, and it was time for him to "take it by force". As the Scriptures tell us, "There was a long war between the house of Saul and the house of David; and David grew stronger and stronger, while the house of Saul became weaker and weaker" (2 Sam 3:1).

It is interesting to note the order of events that led from David as shepherd-boy to David as God-appointed leader of a united and powerful Israel. (For this will essentially be the same path that many end-time Davids will travel also). For David, God's first school of preparation was shepherding a small flock of sheep - an ideal training ground for later leadership. Here, David learnt to faithfully care for those he had been given charge over, and to defend them fearlessly from the ravaging 'bears and lions', etc. As Jesus said centuries later, "You have been faithful over a little, I will set you over much" (Mt 25:21).

It was now that David received his first 'kingly' anointing, by the hands of the prophet Samuel. He then burst onto the public scene in quite spectacular fashion (the victory over Goliath), but quickly found himself offside with the existing leadership, and was forced into hiding, along with his small band of outcasts. All this time, God was testing and preparing him for the great task ahead. This period of agonized "waiting" in the wilderness went on for years. Finally, with Saul 'dead', David received his second kingly anointing, and became king of Judah, from whence he waged war on the "house of Saul" for leadership of the whole nation of Israel.

David was finally anointed as leader of all Israel some years later. Under his leadership, Israel became a united, powerful, victorious nation, mighty in battle and utterly glorifying to God - displaying His grace and glory to all nations. This is exactly what the coming move of God must bring about also. All of this is the exact purpose and reason for the coming Reformation and Revival. Glory to God! Jesus is returning for a Bride that is "without spot or wrinkle or any such thing."

One of the things that I most want people to take note of in the story of David and Saul is the vital importance of waiting for GOD'S PERFECT TIME AND FOR HIS ANOINTING before we move. We see this principle so clearly in the life of David. This is why I want to encourage all of you who are reading this to WAIT UNTIL GOD MOVES before you try "pulling down the old", etc. We must await His perfect time.

I BELIEVE IN LEADERS!

Something I want to establish very strongly here is that the coming new leaders must never be afraid to truly "LEAD" God's people. If God appoints you to lead, then LEAD!

Over the last ten years or so, I have often moved in circles in which it has been emphasized that any future Revival must have "no superstars and no personalities". Sounds good! Obviously, all the glory must go to God, and self-promotion, pride and the idolizing of human leadership must have no place. But very often, I have found that this whole "no superstars, no personalities" thing has been taken much further, into the realm of basically desiring that there be no real leaders at all. So what do we actually mean by this? Do we mean to say that God is now finished with "men of valor" - the Joshuas, the Gideons, the Peters or the Pauls of ages past? Are we really now to have a kind of "leaderless" Revival, as some have stated? (Declaring that God has little need for real leaders at all, and that He Himself will do all the leading, with almost no requirement for earthly shepherds). Sounds so right, doesn't it? So "spiritual" - so democratic. No superstars and no personalities. You have to admit, it has a nice ring to it.

The only problem is, if you take this concept to it's logical conclusion, then you have to do away with almost every major form of ministry found in the Bible – both Old and New Testaments. If God had operated this way in the past, then there would never have been a Moses or a Joshua, a Gideon or a Sampson, a David or a John-the-Baptist, a Peter or a Paul, a Martin Luther or a John Wesley, a William Booth or a Charles Finney (etc, etc, etc...) No heroes, no leaders, no apostles, no 5-fold ministry, no "mighty men of valor" to lead God's people into war. For what use does God have of such men, when He can lead the people Himself? All of the men we have just mentioned were God's "heroes" of their day - leaders whom God had raised up into a place of prominence to lead His people, usually after secretly training them for years in the 'wilderness'. And it has to be said: Every one of them was a "strong" (not insipid) type of leader - because that is exactly what God had raised them up to be. (This is not to say that leaders should ever "lord it over" the people. Absolutely not! But they must possess true godly authority – along with genuine meekness).

Let me ask you this question: Can we even have New Testament Christianity without the "5-fold" leadership of Ephesians 4 – building up the church? Is it even possible? Would there have been any Book of Acts without the apostles? Didn't the early church "devote" itself to the apostles' teaching? If there are no shepherds, teachers, evangelists, prophets or apostles, how can the Body possibly be built up into the "full stature" described in Eph 4:11-13?

For me personally, this whole question has been one that I have pondered at length over the years. And I have to admit that during that time, what God has shown me has caused me to adopt the exact opposite position to that which I formerly held. I can no longer believe in a "leaderless" Revival. Everything that I have ever read about past moves of God, from the beginning of the Old Testament right down through recent Revival history has convinced me that this whole "leaderless" concept is a dangerous fallacy. Not only is it almost entirely lacking in reason or historical legitimacy, but it actually goes against the very character of God and His dealings with men right down through the ages. For God has ALWAYS USED MEN AND WOMEN as His instruments to bring repentance, deliverance or Revival to His people, and as carriers of His anointing - displaying His glory to a dying world. And He has always raised up STRONG LEADERS to establish and carry forward almost every new move that He has visited upon the earth. I am convinced that He is about to do so again, in the coming Reformation.

A true Revival leader must never be 'soft' or compromising, but neither must he be harsh or authoritarian. He must be both a strong and a loving man of God,- wise, patient, "apt to teach", but also not afraid to "reprove, rebuke and exhort" where necessary. Above all else, in these mild and insipid times, HE MUST NOT BE AFRAID TO BE A TRUE LEADER, despite what people say. History clearly demonstrates that with an absence of strong leadership, the devil gets in so fast that the coming move of God would probably only last a matter of months (if that).

What happened to the 1904 Welsh Revival after Evan Roberts (who was without a doubt one of God's great Revivalists) suddenly disappeared from the scene, should be an object lesson to us all. Within a very short space of time after he was gone, the whole Revival was being absolutely taken apart by the enemy, with no-one else around with the respect or authority to correct the excesses, expose the counterfeits, and keep the whole thing on the rails. It seems that Evan Roberts (whose Revival preaching was being reported by secular newspapers around the world at that time) had been persuaded by certain parties that his prominence in the Revival was somehow "stealing glory away from God". So, as a truly humble man, he took what he obviously thought was the most 'humble' or spiritual option available - he hid himself away in a small house, and refused to see anyone or to preach again for many years.

Thus, with God's true "strongman" gone (the one man with the true mantle and anointing, raised up by God to lead the Revival), the devil now had free reign to 'spoil his goods'. In many ways this disaster could be likened to the children of Israel suddenly losing Moses after crossing the Red Sea, or losing Joshua just as they entered the promised land. The result was entirely predictable. Chaos! The devil had an absolute field-day, and the famous Welsh Revival, which should have been one of God's enduring victories, ended in relative ignominy after little more than one year. Excesses and counterfeits flooded in, and thousands of young converts fell away (though many thousands still remained, and some new Pentecostal groups were able to emerge - so not all was lost).

I hope I am not being ungracious to the memory of one of God's great Revivalists here. Please believe me, I hold Evan Roberts in the highest regard. But I believe it is very important that we learn the lessons from this, and other moves of God down through history. The simple fact of the matter is: NO LEADERS - NO REVIVAL. If those whom God is calling to be leaders of a new move of God fail to truly "LEAD" it, then the devil is able to very easily undermine or destroy what God is doing. It is not "humble" to refuse to take authority and be a strong leader when God is calling you to do so - it is simply irresponsible and disobedient. And the same will be true of the coming move of God also. This is the exact reason why God is about to raise up so many currently-hidden "men of authority" (apostles and prophets, etc), as leaders of the coming great move.

The Revivals under Luther, Wesley and Booth were also quite significant in this regard. They were not perfect, but at least the leaders recognized the need for constant strong leadership. This is no doubt one reason why these particular Revivals lasted as long as they did. (Another reason is that they were "outward looking" - taking the Revival anointing out onto the streets - especially Wesley and Booth. They also had a 'new wineskin' - new leaders, new structures, etc. All of these things were key factors).

The coming Reformation/ Revival will need strong leaders right from the start. And no doubt God has a hidden supply of these (as always), ready to take the field at His command. I also believe that in the coming move, new converts will grow up and fulfill their potential in God very rapidly. New ministries will arise and mature at a startling rate. He will raise up both the very young and the very old. After all, isn't this maturing of new, vigorous, anointed ministries one of the very reasons why God appoints leaders in His church (to bring them to maturity)? True leadership of God's flock has clearly always been a great privilege, but also an awesome responsibility.

WALKING IN POWER

Personally I can no longer believe in a church that does not openly glorify Jesus Christ on the streets of every city. I cannot believe in a church that is so bereft of the genuine MIRACLE-working power of God, as that which we call the "church" today. Where are the Elijahs of God? Why do we seem so satisfied merely to watch as the world goes to hell all around us? I can frankly no longer believe in a "church" in which Jesus lies 'wounded in the house of His friends'.

The Church I believe in is an invading force, a rampaging army, that cuts a swathe over the whole earth, "destroying the works of the devil". It is a people of great faith and ruthless determination, who batter down every 'gate' of hell and utterly destroy every stronghold, so that the oppressed might be liberated and the captives be set free. This will be a 'Joshua' army, commissioned by God to "take the land", to raze every work of Satan to the ground and slaughter every living thing in the enemy camp. Like Jesus, they will "set their faces as flint" toward the Holy City, and nothing will stand in their path.

In saying all of this, however, I want to make it clear that I am not speaking here of "taking over" the earth's political and educational systems, etc. This teaching (which is known as Dominion Theology) is quite widespread in some circles. However, the war that I am talking about is an entirely "SPIRITUAL" one - a war for the hearts and the minds of men. It is certainly not a war for control of the world's secular institutions (for, as Jesus clearly stated, "My kingdom is not of this world" - Jn 18:36). The purpose of the battle that is about to be waged will be to expose and destroy the lies that bind the people, and to bring down the 'principalities and powers' that hold them captive. Destroying every spiritual "work" and falsehood of the devil - that's what this is all about.

THE REFINING OF THE DAVIDS

In closing this chapter, I would just like to return briefly to our analogy of the Sauls, the Jonathans and the Davids. There can be no doubt that God has been preparing a "David company" of leaders to arise and lead His people in the coming move - leaders after His own heart who have been in hidden preparation for years. However, a large number of these David-type ministries will probably have been badly stung by some of their dealings with the present Saulish system. As I have said, the Davids will almost always feel like misfits in the current church set-up. They are essentially designed to fit into the revived church of tomorrow rather than the Laodicean church of today.

Some of them will have received such a hammering whenever they have dared to speak up in the past, that they have now become quite 'crushed' and hesitant about sharing their convictions. Others will be feeling rather lonely - wondering if they are the only ones in their church who feel the way they do about the state of things. There will be others again who, like David, have felt compelled to withdraw from the current system altogether, to a place of refuge far away from the Sauls. Still others may have felt called into the 'wilderness', just so that they can spend time alone with God, learning from Him. Believe me, I can sympathize with all of these. However, I also believe that it is extremely vital that the Davids deal with any hurts, resentments, bitterness, rejection, or rebellion that have found a place in their hearts due to their unhappy dealings with the churches, or other authorities. Not only is this vitally important, but it is also URGENT I believe, because God is going to want to use these 'David' ministries in a great way very soon. For if the refining process is not complete, how can they hope to be a part of what God is about to do?

Every one of us needs to search our hearts to make sure that there is no deep root of resentment or rebellion lurking within us, as a result of our past dealings with authority figures (pastors, parents, etc), or other Christians. We need to be extremely thorough and totally honest with ourselves. We must not make excuses. We must deal with the root of the problem. Past wounds and resentments, etc, can have a tremendous effect on our present attitudes towards authority. These kinds of bad experiences can cause us to become "reactionary" - still reacting against these wounds many years later. This is often the source of "rebellion" in many peoples' hearts. If we are 'prophetic', then such wounds will almost certainly harshly distort many of our prophetic words. (In fact, it has been truly said that many false prophets are really true prophets with "unhealed wounds"). It is vital that we search our hearts, and deal with these deep roots or strongholds in our lives as urgently as possible (for they can seep poison right through every part of our lives, if we are not careful).

Here are some sure signs of "rebellion" in a person's life: They secretly enjoy hearing or seeing authority figures or institutions mocked or made a fool of. They can't seem to help 'murmuring' or complaining to others against particular authority figures that they know. They enjoy deliberately speaking or acting (or even dressing) in such a way that will shock the "establishment". (MOTIVES are the things that need to be looked at here). This list could go on and on, but I am sure you get the idea. "REBELLION" - a truly subtle yet deadly sin (and one of Satan's all-time favorites).

How do we deal with such roots of rebellion deep within us? In exactly the same way as we deal with roots or strongholds of any other kind: We ask God to shed light on them, and then utterly 'RENOUNCE' them in the name of Jesus Christ, not just with our words, but also from the depths of our very being. We repent of them (with genuine godly sorrow) and COMMAND them gone in Jesus' name. One thing that true godly sorrow and deep repentance will always produce is a genuine HATRED OF SIN, and this will bring abundant 'good fruit' into our lives.

As I said before, honoring and respecting authority does not necessarily mean abject, unthinking "submission" towards our leaders. We are still all individually responsible for our own walk before God, and we need to be sure that our leaders are not leading us astray. If they are leading us into serious deception, then God will often expect us to make a stand and say something about it. If this is done in the right spirit, then it is certainly not "rebellion". However, if the deception continues, then after making our stand known, the best thing to do would probably be to leave that particular group (unless God tells us to stay). We are not to be unthinking 'slaves' to authority, but neither are we to ever be found amongst the rebellious "murmurers and complainers". God will help us judge what is right, if our hearts are pure before him. We are certainly not obliged to be loyal to any man who is leading us into blatant deception. Really, I guess the best policy always is "BALANCE IN ALL THINGS".

And just a short word here about the (often young) harsh, immature "prophet"-types who go around "blasting" people with bludgeoning, judgmental prophecies, etc. (I used to be one of these myself, some years ago!) Often, such 'prophets' may have a true calling on their life, but their immaturity, their (unknowing) pride and arrogance, and their secret rebellion make them very dangerous to themselves and to others. Until they allow God to bring true brokenness and humility into their lives (an often painful process), then they will usually end up causing more harm than good wherever they go. There is a time for "rebuking" (though only experienced ministries should ever really consider it), but most of the time, there is no substitute for "speaking the truth in love". Wisdom, patience, gentleness meekness and love should all be part of the 'strength' that God has built into our ministries. Otherwise we can end up doing great damage to His precious sheep. (For words can inflict great harm). Please think and pray about these things, my friends?

CHAPTER FIVE

A GREAT "YOUTH" REVIVAL?

Some of the strongest and most persistent prophecies about Revival in the West say that it will be a YOUTH Revival as well as a Great Reformation. But for this to happen, today's "entertain them at all costs" approach to youth ministry would have to be utterly overthrown. We must do away with "entertain, entertain, entertain." Instead the youth will have to be shown a cause worth dying for.

Think for a minute of the "Commando Army" prophecy that we looked at earlier. In discussing ways that we can 'survive' the current economic crisis, one way should have become obvious by now: We can survive the crisis by becoming such radical disciples of Jesus that he drafts us into His commandos! This may sound frivolous, but it is absolutely true. There is no safe place in such a storm except at the very center of God's will. I am convinced that only radical disciples of Jesus stand the best chance. They will survive and thrive while others who depend on earthly tactics and fleshly means will utterly fail. So if you want to "survive the Depression" - get radical for Christ!

One of the best examples we have of a real "Commando Army" is the early Salvation Army of 130 years ago. In fact, the astounding history of the early Salvationists has to be heard to be believed.

When it started, the Salvation Army was surely the most extreme Street holiness movement in the history of the church (though who would know it today?) The year 1878 saw the birth of one of the most outrageous, zealous and anointed Revival movements that the world has ever known. Made up mostly of young zealots and led by a spiritual dynamo named William Booth, this was God's answer when extreme measures were called for to combat the apathy and spiritual torpor of the times.

Originally named simply the 'Christian Mission', Booth's movement always had a 'Revival' feel about it. But it wasn't until they went "military" in 1878 that the whole thing exploded worldwide. This was no longer simply home-missionary work. It was holy guerrilla warfare against darkness and the devil. Booth's motto was:- "Go for souls and go for the worst". It was nothing less than all-out war.

Within five years of becoming a military-style 'Army', Booth's fifty mission stations had become 634 army corps (106 of them overseas). These soldiers were some of the most innovative, daring and war-like disciples of Jesus that had ever walked the earth. There was much opposition. In the year 1882 alone in England, 669 Salvationists were physically assaulted, 56 Army buildings were wholly or partially wrecked, "skeleton armies" of local thugs were formed to attack the Salvationists, and 86 Salvation Army soldiers were thrown into prison for causing a disturbance on the streets. There were literally street-riots almost everywhere they went. And they were front-page news around the world. But all the while, thousands were being transformed. The common people, the poor, the orphans, the drunkards, the brawlers, the thugs - people who never went near a church - were being converted in their droves.

The Salvationists became well-known for their rather raucous brass band music (which was the loudest street-music around at the time) as well as their fiery Repentance preaching. It was quite common for them to form brass bands out of instruments held together by bits of string, and with musicians who could hardly even play! One eyewitness described the noise as sounding "like a brass band that has gone out of it's mind." They often used the popular drinking songs and pub songs of the day, changing the words to make them into battle hymns or worship songs. As William Booth said, "Why should the devil have all the best music?" (A saying also credited to Martin Luther and John Wesley in their day. They all used the world's music the same way!)

The early Salvation Army were truly outrageous by the Victorian standards of the day - in fact by any standards. But while respectable church people were often scandalized, thousands upon thousands of sinners were converted - usually from the lowest sectors of society that Jesus Himself had ministered to.

Then as today, the Salvationists waged a war on poverty and hunger wherever they went. Like the apostles, it was not just evangelism they were interested in - it was transformation of the whole person - spirit, soul and body. The Salvation Army became known around the world for it's practical help of the poor and needy, just like the early church.

With their "BLOOD AND FIRE" flags, and their uniforms similar to the war uniforms of the day, these were God's spiritual assault commandos - fearless and radical evangelists for Jesus. It was not uncommon for them to pray all night and preach all day. They were very much a YOUTH MOVEMENT. (Even their Officers were often only in their late teens or twenties).

There is no doubt that tremendous courage and DARING will be required by those who seek to become part of such a 'Street-Revival' today. For the modern church has grown fat and the devil has been winning the war for the hearts and minds of our youth for decades. But I believe that indeed such "daring" ones will be found. And there will need to be "mothers and fathers" in such a movement too (though they will need to be just as 'radical' as the youth).

We stand on the edge of the most momentous days in the history of the church, my friends. I believe there is an "explosion" coming. Are you truly ready for the coming Reformation to turn into a 'Street-Revival'? Are you ready for the "Commando Army"?

"TO THE YOUTH OF AMERICA"

I wrote the following several years ago, calling the Christian youth to become truly "extreme" in their radical commitment to Christ:

"I write this as a musician and a radical. Christian Youth of America, your generation is dying, and I need to ask if you are EXTREME enough to provide the answers. We know there never was anyone more "Extreme" than Jesus. But what about you?

Christian Youth, I need to ask why you sit in the padded pews of your fathers while all around the darkness takes your cities and your friends.

I need to ask why you worship the great god of Entertainment, just like your parents before you - but a bit 'louder' - and think that is "radical".

I need to ask why you think it is "extreme" to slam and mosh, when all the while the devil owns your streets, and fat Record Companies line their pockets with your cash.

I need to know why you have allowed the system to make you a slave - a "consumer" - a clone. I need to know why you can be sucked into buying $150 shoes and $200 sunglasses - while 30,000 children die of starvation every day.

I need to know why you will not cry out to the rich money-preachers "REPENT". I need to know why you still enjoy it when they tickle your ears and never speak of Hell. I need to know why you accept it when their gospel sounds like a toothpaste commercial - all slick and no substance. Well-dressed clones with plastic smiles, selling you the latest line in snake-oil. WHEN WILL YOU WEEP?

I look at your piercings and your tattoos and your hair and I still have to tell you: You are nowhere near EXTREME ENOUGH. The outward appearance will not do.

The time is coming when an army of young warriors will hit the streets - fearless and bold beyond anything we have ever seen. Even death itself will hold no fear. They will cry to the church "REPENT" and to the comfortable, "SELL what you have and GIVE TO THE POOR". They will be hated and despised by religious authorities. They will openly decry the TV preachers and eschew the watered-down pap that passes for 'gospel' in our day. They will reject sin and love people - even the homeless and the very least. Utterly pure of heart, they will befriend the prostitutes and the gang bangers. They will look and sound just like Jesus.

With great daring and ruthless aggression, this army will make war on the devil and the darkness. Their music will be hymns of battle. Their sound will ROAR over the crowd. Truly these shall be the 'Sons of Thunder'.

Christian Youth of America, can you not hear the call of God in this hour? All heaven awaits the moment when you will arise and ACT on behalf of your generation.

To the Christian Youth of America I say:

It is time to get "EXTREME"."

CHAPTER SIX

TWO KEYS TO "PERSONAL REVIVAL"

For Christians to truly prepare themselves to have a part in real Reformation and Revival, one of the most obvious prerequisites is that they have to come into a state of "personal Revival" themselves. The two key questions that we will be covering in this chapter are: (1) How do I get into this state of "Personal Revival", and (2) How do we get from there into "Corporate Revival"?

I am writing this as someone who has studied Revival history for many years. I have looked at Revivals from recent decades and Revivals from centuries ago. And after all this study, I have found that there seem to be two major secrets to obtaining real Revival – including "personal" Revival in our own lives.

These things are: (1) Extremely deep REPENTANCE, and (2) A kind of "wrestling, agonizing" PRAYER - crying to God for the 'outpouring' of His Holy Spirit.

These two things have been the secrets to countless Revivals down the ages - and I truly believe they will be so again. That is why there is nothing more important that we can be discussing right now.

ACTUALLY EXPERIENCING DEEP REPENTANCE

As Frank Bartleman (from the 'Azusa Street' Revival) wrote: "I received from God early in 1905 the following keynote to revival: 'The DEPTH of revival will be determined exactly by the DEPTH of the spirit of REPENTANCE.' And this will obtain for all people, at all times."

I can confirm that all history backs up Bartleman's words here. And I can also tell you that if you want to get into a truly "Revived" state -or a state of "personal Revival" - then DEEP Repentance is one of the keys.

What we often find is that Christians have turned away from a lot of the "obvious" sins, such as lying, stealing, adultery, etc. But there are other things that they are aware of in their lives that are not right. It is dealing with these "other things" that can be the key to a far greater intimacy with God.

Do you know that God HATES all sin, and that when you get close to God then your heart will HATE sin just like He does?

So let's get "practical" with this. Here is what you need to do to deal with these things at a deep level: Firstly, get off by yourself with God. You need time alone in a quiet place with Him. Secondly, ask and plead with God to "shine His light" into your heart, to show you any unclean thing, whether it be unforgiveness, lust, speaking against people behind their backs, holding grudges, little "white" lies, etc. Ask God to show you how HE FEELS about sin. Ask Him to shine this light deep inside you and show you things that you need to confess and renounce and ask forgiveness for. In some cases, you may need to go to a brother or sister and apologize to them or even make restitution. Make sure the repentance goes to the DEEPEST LEVEL possible. Confess each sin specifically to God, turn from it and ask God to cleanse you. With a lot of people it is these so-called "MINOR SINS" that are holding them back.

Here is one last quote on this subject from Evan Roberts of the Welsh Revival: "First, is there any sin in your past with which you have not honestly dealt,- not confessed to God? On your knees at once. Your past must be put away and cleansed. Second, is there anything in your life that is doubtful - anything you cannot decide whether it is good or evil? Away with it. There must not be a trace of a cloud between you and God. Have you forgiven everybody - EVERYBODY? If not, don't expect forgiveness for your sins..." [Source: David Matthews, "I Saw the Welsh Revival", pg 81].

This issue of TRULY forgiving those who have hurt you can be a big one. It is important to be BRUTALLY HONEST with yourself. Is there still "bad feeling" deep inside you towards certain people? Is there a trace of bitterness when you speak about that person? We all need to get before God and repent and RENOUNCE all unforgiveness from deep within us. Going through this whole "deep repentance" process is the first key to personal Revival.

A 15-YEAR-OLD EXPERIENCES "PERSONAL REVIVAL"

A couple of years ago a teenager named Lauren from the USA sent me the following email:

"Bro. Andrew...

I am about to be 15 and my entire life I thought I was saved. I've grown up in a Christian home. I knew the word and I heard pretty correct things all my life and thought I was OK because I "asked Jesus to come into my heart" when I was 3 and I was baptized around 11. I believe God did something in me. I've spoken in tongues since I was about 4 ½.

I had gotten a hold of your teaching "How to Experience Personal Revival". I had listened to it about 10 times and thought it was great. Well on June 1st after talking to one of my very close friends about her experience with making a list like you said, I decided to take notes. Earlier that week I had begun to have these weird questions like, "Am I REALLY saved?"

Well, I took notes on that teaching and I'm telling you, I HEARD what you said. My heart heard it. Not just my ears. It was like a massive revelation - like an entire new gospel I had never heard before. You made a comment, "If you're not living in revived Christianity, what makes you think you're living in Christianity?" The more I thought about it, the more I realized that I had never been truly "saved".

My whole life I had struggled with sin thinking that I had repented of it only to find myself the next day repenting of it again. It wasn't true repentance! TO CHANGE THE WAY YOU THINK. I had made everything so complicated! The simplicity of the gospel is so alive in my heart and mind. Anyway, it was like I got a small understanding of the holiness of God and he was someone I had never met before. I made a list like you said, and I poured my heart out to this holy God and asked him to take the biggest search light he had and show me anything that was displeasing to him and I repented of it immediately. After I did that I felt utterly different. Like a weight I had had my entire life that I didn't even know about was gone. It's like the sky is bluer and the grass is greener and the birds sing louder just because I know the true Jesus. I know that this is real. It's not like before. I woke up the next morning and it was still there. And the next, it was still there, and last week - it was still there!... This past Sunday I actually got baptized in my next door neighbors' backyard. -All I want to do is approach my holy God with only the holiness He can give. And walk completely and utterly transparent before Him..."

Please notice two crucial points in the above email: (1) That it was a revelation of God's utter HOLINESS and hatred for sin that helped Lauren to truly repent before Him; and (2) That she made a "LIST" of every possible sin (major and minor) that she saw in her life – and systematically went through that List, repenting of each thing before God, one by one. No wonder she experienced such a breakthrough! And cannot the same thing happen for every person reading this book? What are you waiting for?

KEY # 2 - "WRESTLING, AGONIZING" PRAYER

When you study history, you soon notice that there is a specific type of prayer that you see in Revivals again and again. When I first began to study past moves of God I quickly realized this, because I came across it so often. This special type of prayer is an ESSENTIAL ingredient of Revival.

The old Revivalists used to speak of having the "spirit of prayer". They spoke of weeping, agonizing, pleading, wrestling, 'travailing' in prayer. The whole reason that these Revival preachers were so anointed and saturated with the presence of God was because they had truly broken through, right into His very throneroom in prayer, and had spent much time communing with Him there. This type of praying has always been one of the most important keys to true Revival.

Frank Bartleman wrote: "God wonderfully met and assured us as we wrestled with Him for the outpouring of His Spirit upon the people. My life was by this time literally swallowed up in prayer." And D.M. McIntyre wrote: "Before the great revival in Gallneukirchen broke out, Martin Boos spent hours and days and often nights in lonely agonies of intercession. Afterwards, when he preached, his words were as flame, and the hearts of the people as grass."

As was said of the great Welsh Revivalist Evan Roberts: "He would break down, crying bitterly for God to bend them, in an agony of prayer, the tears coursing down his cheeks, with his whole frame writhing." And John Wesley asked: "Have you any days of fasting and prayer? Storm the throne of grace and persevere therein, and mercy will come down." Brothers, sisters, we need to get DESPERATE in our praying!

HOW TO "WRESTLE" IN PRAYER

Now, it is very important to realize that this type of prayer is not just for "special" people or leaders. It is absolutely one of the keys to "personal Revival" for every one of us. The Bible makes it very clear that the "effectual fervent prayer of a righteous man" is available to us all.

And history shows that "wrestling Revival prayer" can actually be TAUGHT to Christians. This comes through loud and clear in the book 'Anointed for Burial', which is Todd and DeAnn Burke's account of the mighty Revival in Cambodia in the 1970's. It occurred when God had already been moving there for some time.

Todd wrote: "Referring to Genesis 32, I told them how Jacob WRESTLED with the Lord until He blessed him. 'If we expect power and blessing from the Lord, we are going to have to be willing to wrestle with Him in prayer and fasting, in self-denial, in taking up our cross,' I said. Then I shared with them from a devotional book by Hudson Taylor, "An easy-going, non-self-denying life will never be one of power." With that, everyone began to wrestle in prayer, and before long, the blessing came."

When these people broke up into prayer groups and began to "wrestle" with God in prayer as Todd had taught them, the result was actual "OUTPOURINGS" of the Holy Spirit. (ie. The Holy Spirit descending upon whole groups of Christians just like in Acts, with incredibly powerful results). It was an amazing time.

Notice that these Christians were actually TAUGHT to "wrestle" with God in this way. And they simply went and did it! Early in the 1904 Welsh Revival, Evan Roberts taught the children of Moriah to pray this simple prayer: "Send the Spirit to Moriah for Jesus Christ's sake." Later, he developed this same concept for his general meetings - because it was vital that people plead with God to "send His Spirit" down upon them.

After all, this is exactly what Pentecost was all about! It was the 120 in the upper room, crying out to God for ten days, and then God "sending His Spirit" like a mighty rushing wind, and filling them to overflowing. In the past 50 years, there have been many powerful Revivals in which God outpoured His Spirit in a similar way. When God "outpours" His Spirit like this, it is far more than a person simply being baptized in the Spirit. It is a general "outpouring".

In fact, an "Outpouring of the Holy Spirit" is the essence of what Revival truly is. And just like Pentecost, the result is that many become FILLED with the Holy Spirit, and many others become greatly CONVICTED of their sin. True Revival is the Glory of God coming down. It is His Spirit being "POURED OUT" in a specific place or upon a specific people. We need to 'wrestle' with God to see such an outpouring occur in our day.

Now, before you can 'wrestle' with God in prayer, here is what you need to do: (1) Become DESPERATE to see God GLORIFIED in the earth; (2) Cleanse your "hands" and your "heart" so that you can truly enter into the throneroom of God; (3) Plead with God to outpour His "spirit of prayer" upon you; (4) Nurture His "fire" in your heart, so that you can 'agonize' in prayer before Him. (5) When you do pray, be very SPECIFIC in pleading with God to outpour His Spirit upon yourself as well as a specific group or place. We all need this fresh infilling.

If you can do these simple things, then today is the day when you can begin to "wrestle" with God in prayer. Do not delay. This could be the key to seeing you transformed by "personal Revival" and coming into a far deeper communion with God.

FROM PERSONAL TO "CORPORATE"

Having studied Revivals now for over 20 years, I am convinced that the road to "personal Revival" is really the same as the road to 'corporate Revival'. The major keys have always been "deep repentance" and agonizing prayer for more of God's SPIRIT. Our motives for seeking God must never be selfish ones. We should be seeking Him for His own sake, not for what we can "get out of it". It is to SEE HIM GLORIFIED that we ask these things.

So, my friends, all I can do is urge you to get into a quiet place and give yourself to heart-searching repentance and "agonizing" prayer until you see a massive "breakthrough" in your Christian walk. We all need to be filled with His Spirit again and again. Since I was 17 years old, I would attribute many spiritual breakthroughs in my life to these two Revival secrets. They have truly revolutionized my life.

So what about "Corporate" Revival - where God's Spirit is poured out upon whole communities and cities? Well, what God will often do is what He did at Pentecost. He will take His "Revived" ones and use them to bring Revival to others. In other words, if God can find a GROUP of people who have gone through "personal

Revival", then He can use them to speak Truth and carry His anointing into whole areas. And to PRAY for further outpourings.

So what does God need to find in the earth today? Simply GROUPS of "Revived" Christians who can begin to preach repentance and pray for God's Spirit to be outpoured. It all starts with people who have been "Revived".

Evan Roberts' advice for obtaining Revival was as follows: "Congregate the people together who are willing to make a total surrender. Pray and wait. Believe God's promises. Hold daily meetings. May God bless you…"

And as A.T. Pierson wrote, "From the day of Pentecost, there has been not one great spiritual awakening in any land which has not begun in a union of prayer, though only among two or three; no such outward, upward movement has continued after such prayer meetings declined."

CHAPTER SEVEN
THE WORD & THE SPIRIT JOINED

Even though I speak in 'tongues' and believe in all the gifts of the Holy Spirit, there is no doubt that I am far more known as a 'word' preacher than any kind of miracle-worker. For years and years I have prayed for a 'Revival' anointing on my preaching like the Finneys, the Wesleys and the Whitefields of old. But I am well aware that this is only half the story. As Revival history shows, the anointed 'word' by itself can have tremendous power to convict and transform lives. But without MIRACLES I have to question whether we really are representing full New Testament Christianity. I am totally convinced that we must have BOTH - the 'WORD' and the "MIGHTY DEMONSTRATION" of God's holy power.

In 1947 Smith Wigglesworth gave a prophecy about three coming moves of God. Concerning the last (and greatest) of these he said:

"When the new church phase is on the wane, there will be evidence in the churches of something that has not been seen before: a coming together of those with an emphasis on the word and those with an emphasis on the Spirit. When the word and the Spirit come together, there will be the biggest move of the Holy Spirit that the nation, and indeed, the world has ever seen. It will mark the beginning of a revival that will eclipse anything that has been witnessed within these shores, even the Wesleyan and Welsh revivals of former years...."

There it is- "The word and the Spirit" joined.

Let me ask a simple question: What did people "see" when they came across Jesus' ministry? They saw a simple, piercing gospel being preached and also the 'kingdom' being demonstrated through healings and miracles. That is basically what they saw. And what did people "see" in the ministry of the apostles and evangelists of Acts? They saw the same thing. An anointed, piercing gospel and mighty demonstrations of God's power - both together. In fact, we should really ask ourselves - Is it possible to preach the gospel (in the full New Testament sense) without healings and miracles? If we are being truly scriptural, surely we would have to answer- "NO, IT IS NOT."

Another question- Why is the casting out of demons so important in demonstrating the 'kingdom'? Well - what it is showing is the greater AUTHORITY found in the name and the 'king-ship' of Jesus Christ. Even demons have to obey Him! Suddenly everyone sees this beyond a doubt when a demon is cast out before their eyes. I remember the first time I saw this happen as a teenager - before I was a true Christian. The person screamed and writhed as the demon was cast out - just like in the Bible. And what was the result in me? CONVICTION! Suddenly everything in Scripture came alive! Suddenly it was all COMPLETELY REAL! I felt like running forward and surrendering to God on the spot.

And this is why I have to question the casting out of demons in a "back room" somewhere. Notice that Jesus never did this. He cast out demons in PUBLIC - so that the 'kingdom' was demonstrated and God was glorified. Notice too, the absence of "3 hour marathons" in casting out demons in the Bible. They had the anointing and authority from God - and deliverance was mostly quick and decisive.

We have got to see the "Word and the Spirit joined" like this in our own day. I believe God greatly desires it – and if there is to be one last Great Reformation and Revival before the end, I'm sure this is His perfect plan for the End Time church. The piercing preaching of a Charles Finney or a John Wesley - married to the healings and miracles of a Smith Wigglesworth or a John G. Lake. Now THAT I would love to see! Powerful 'word' type ministry joined to powerful "Holy Spirit" type miracles. The very essence of what we find in the Book of Acts. Bring it on, Lord!

RADICAL VISIONS OF REFORMATION

As you know, we have not just spent this book discussing how to "Survive the Depression" – the most important aspect of which is to experience a spiritual revival. (Though this may not seem the most "practical" preparation – in actual fact it is). What we have also been discussing is a much wider picture – a worldwide "shaking" affecting entire nations – and a massive Reformation of the church. Clearly it is through "great tribulation" that we must enter the kingdom.

Let us now focus a little more closely on this great shaking of the church – from the point of view of some very insightful visions and dreams that I came across years ago and published in my 1996 book, "The Coming Great Reformation". I had collected these dreams and visions from prophets and intercessors in my home nation of New Zealand. But they have a "truth" about them that crosses all boundaries.

It is important to note that all over the world in the last 25 years or so, God has been speaking of the great "shaking" and Reformation that are about to come upon His church. For instance, in 1982 a well-known intercessor/ pastor from America was clearly spoken to by God in a powerful visitation: "I am going to change the understanding and expression of Christianity IN THE EARTH in one generation". This is exactly what is about to occur, I believe. God is about to restore us back to the pattern, the purity and the power of the early church. Today we have a "meetings and buildings" oriented church, a church that is hidden away in 'boxes' from the eyes of the world. But all that is about to change.

The following vision is probably one of the most well-known that has ever come out of New Zealand. It was given to an experienced NZ prophet late in 1993 – a man with many years of Christian ministry behind him. He told me that this particular vision was probably the most powerful he had ever had. It unfolded before his eyes like a movie in technicolor, with God speaking to him about aspects of it as he watched.

Here is what he saw:

Basically, it was a traditional wedding scene. The radiantly beautiful Bride had just stepped out of the Cathedral and was standing on the top step, just outside. My friend was told that the Bride was LEAVING 'CHRISTENDOM' (AND ALL THAT GOES WITH IT) FOREVER, leaving the church "system" behind. The Groom (who was Jesus) took her arm, so that He could lead her down and proudly display His beautiful Bride to all the world.

Still inside the Cathedral were all the relatives (these were the various 'streams' and denominations of the church as we know it). Suddenly, while the Bride was still on the top step, an invisible hand gave her a beautiful lily (which had been plucked out by the roots). This was her bridal 'bouquet' (her new anointing?) and for some reason it seemed to be given to her rather late. She threw this bouquet backwards, and some of her relatives in the church, who had been watching her with great jealousy and awe, made a grab for the bouquet. Two of them seemed to snatch it up, but there was a lot of squabbling and pushing amongst them - fighting to be somehow near the Bride or to grab the bouquet. The Groom then led His Bride down the steps and through the huge crowd of cheering people below, who had been unable to get into the Cathedral.

In a later vision, my friend was shown that once they had made their way through this huge throng, the happy couple were then taken away on their honeymoon, which was to last for a thousand years.

My friend later made the following comments about this vision:
"The fighting wedding guests are those within the church who in their hearts are ambitious for titles to impress the body and are caught up seeking the gifts (bouquet anointings) and not the giver. They are involved in grand schemes and politics within the church - and they love 'comfort'. They are those who get close to the Truth but do not want to live the truth.

The Bride - leaving the guests behind - is made up of Christians seeking truth in Jesus alone, no matter the cost, leaving compromise behind and seeking Jesus first before the praises of men."

Obviously, there are some pretty shocking implications to this vision, and it is easy to dismiss them if we do not give it some thought. What are we to make of this - THAT THE BRIDE IS ABOUT TO LEAVE THE "CHURCH SYSTEM" AS WE KNOW IT FOREVER?? What does it mean when it speaks of the Bride leaving 'Christendom' and all its cathedrals behind?

The answers to these questions are very simple. We have already been looking at some of them, in fact. The church system as we know it is still full of the traditions of men. Even in the most modern churches, this is the case. We are nothing like the original church that the apostles founded. We meet in buildings that are the invention of man. We study in Seminaries and receive professional degrees that are the invention of man. We hold 'services' and have leadership structures (the 'One man Pastor' model) that are the invention of man. In every way, we are bereft of the pattern, the purity and the power of the early church. Not only that, but we are UTTERLY DIVIDED as well. We have different "labels" and streams - all competing with one another. How on earth are we going to win the world when our very structures and hierarchies keep us separated like this? Is this the 'ONE BODY' that Christ died for?

The word "Christendom" represents the 'system' that has been built up over the years - and all the man-made "ways of doing things" that go with it. God wants it left behind. It has had its day. It has been holding Him back from doing what He wants to do for far too long. And so Jesus is going to bring His true church - the Bride - out of this "system" forever - and she will never be going back.

THE FLAMING ARROWS

The same prophet was shown another very significant vision around the same time. In it he saw God firing "flaming arrows" into the churches. These were 'on-fire' ministries, speaking the word of God. However, the leaders were rushing around trying to damp down the flames! God then sent a "mighty wind" to fan the flames, and suddenly the doors of the churches burst open and all the people flooded out onto the streets to become one huge throng. I believe that this is an exact picture of what is about to take place.

But notice in this vision that the leaders were 'damping down' what God was trying to do. I find this alarming because in past moves of God some of the worst opposition and persecution has come from the existing leadership. In fact, in the early years of the Salvation Army it was not uncommon for ministers to actually lead violent mobs against their street-meetings! This has been a pattern right down through history.

It is a sad fact that those who have a vested interest in maintaining the status quo will often be violently opposed to any real change taking place. They will often come up with the most "spiritual" sounding reasons for their opposition, but at the end of the day it is usually because they feel 'threatened' or convicted by the new move. Sometimes it is simple jealousy. Many reformers and revivalists such as Martin Luther, John Wesley and William Booth faced enormous opposition from the established church leadership of their day for precisely this reason. That is why true Reformation and Revival are often the most controversial and the most persecuted spiritual events of their time. Sadly, as stated earlier, it has often been the CHRISTIANS (particularly the leaders) who have persecuted new moves of God the worst.

Let us look at another of these NZ visions that gives further insight into what we have been discussing. This one was given to an intercessor that I know who has led a Revival prayer-group in New Zealand for many years. She received this vision while deep in prayer.

The first thing she saw was church buildings of every kind - modern, stained-glass, plain and steepled - every variety you can imagine. This part of the vision was in black and white. The churches all looked abandoned - like a ghost town, with birds nesting in them and doors and windows askew, etc. And in each church, she saw a huge tattered old curtain or 'veil' stretched across the inside.

The second part of the vision was all in color. She saw hundreds of Christians outdoors (with guitars, etc), fellowshipping together in the open air. She knew that these Christians had abandoned their church buildings and 'divisions', and were now fellowshipping freely out-of-doors. When she asked God what the huge tattered curtain in each of the abandoned churches represented, she was told that when Jesus was crucified, the veil/curtain in the temple was rent, thus allowing the people free access to the 'Holy of Holies'. However, the churches had raised up this veil once again. But now these structures had been abandoned, thus allowing the common people free access to God's Holy-of-Holies once more.

What an astounding vision! Yet how tragically true it is. We in the churches have been guilty of raising up all kinds of barriers and obstacles that keep ordinary people from finding or seeing God. A lot of these barriers are because of the 'system' we have built - a system that is supposedly meant to help people approach God - but which in fact does the opposite. It shuts the ordinary people out. But when the Reformation comes, all that is going to change.

As we discussed earlier, just imagine if some miracle occurred, and the church buildings closed down so that all the Spirit-filled Christians in a town simply met together in a local park. Preaching, worship, healing, etc - out in the open air. ALMOST EVERY DAY. And true 'Unity' for once. None of these private little kingdoms.

And imagine if, instead of going to meetings just with people from "your fellowship", you gathered in homes with the LOCAL

Christians from your street. The Lord's Supper, baptisms and spiritual gifts such as tongues, interpretation, prophecy, spiritual songs and teaching occurring in Christians' homes all the time. (1 Cor 14:26). And no "labels" or denominations in sight. Just the LOCAL church in someone's home. What a powerful thing this would be! As we have seen, what I am describing here is EXACTLY WHAT THE EARLY CHURCH WAS LIKE. Large open-air gatherings and small local home-fellowships. It's not too complicated, is it? In fact, it is very simple. In the coming Reformation, this is exactly what we've got to get back to.

As the great Reformer Martin Luther said: "Learn from me, how difficult a thing it is to throw off errors confirmed by the example of all the world, and which, through long habit, have become a second nature to us."

As always, God is going to delight in using the "foolish things of this world to confound the wise" in this Revival. He is going to use the "little" people - the people who are of no account - to humble the powerful, the successful and the mighty. He is going to take the unknowns and the outcasts, the praying solo mothers and the ex-gang-members, the "fishermen and the tax-collectors", and He is going to anoint them and raise them up in ways that were thought impossible. And all they will be interested in doing is glorifying Him in every conceivable way.

When this happens, many of today's leaders will marvel, just as the scribes and Chief Priests marveled at the boldness of Peter and John when they saw that they were "unlearned and ignorant men... and they took knowledge of them, that THEY HAD BEEN WITH JESUS" (Acts 4:13). That is the secret: "They had been with Jesus". And thus it will be of everyone who is used of God in this Revival. "I thank you, O Father, Lord of heaven and earth, because you have hidden these things from the wise and prudent, and have revealed them unto babes" (Mt 11:25).

This much is clear: Jesus must have His virgin Bride. He cannot return until a Bride is prepared for Him that is literally "without spot, or wrinkle, or any such thing". That is what this Revival is all about: To bring into being and display His beautiful Bride to all the earth. In physical terms, this 'Bridal' company of saints will not look particularly amazing or special. Like the original apostles, they will be ordinary people with an extraordinary calling and anointing. Many of them will no-doubt seem a little rough or 'ill-suited' (from an outward point of view) to be endued with such power, but this will only serve to bring God all the more glory. They may not look like much on the outside, but these men and women will have hearts that are literally "as pure as snow". They will be a people who know exactly what it means to walk in total heart purity before God. To Him, they will be vastly more precious than all of the "gold or pearls or costly array" of this entire Universe. And they will go forth with great power, "destroying the works of the devil" in His name.

Sadly, it is my belief that the majority of the current apostolic, prophetic and Charismatic movements are woefully under-prepared for the upheaval that is coming. In fact, it is my belief that very little they have built will survive the massive shaking that has now started. No movement will be immune from the sifting and judgment that I believe God has already begun to visit upon His church.

Tragically, it seems that even many good men involved in these movements have found themselves in the position of 'Jonathans' in the current scenario. In other words, they have become caught between their "reputation" (or position) in the present order of things, and their desire to be part of the coming 'reign of David'. They have a foot in both camps and they are largely acceptable to both. This is a very precarious (and potentially deadly) position to be in. For as we have seen, because Saul is currently in power, it is far easier to stick with him, than with the outcast Davids. Remember, in the Biblical analogy that we discussed earlier, JONATHAN STUCK WITH SAUL TOO LONG, and ended up falling under the SAME JUDGEMENT THAT CAME UPON SAUL. Even though today's Jonathans have certainly been 'friends of the new move of God', it has clearly been far easier for them to stick with Saul than to risk everything and throw in their lot with the Davids. Such Jonathans are surely now in deadly danger.

It is my belief that it will become more and more impossible to steer a "middle course" between what is of Saul and what is of David today. God will bring about a complete 'separation', a total dividing between these two camps, so that all that is of Saul can fall under the sword of His judgment, and all that is of David can go on to "possess the land" in His name.

God has begun to sift and divide His church. And this shaking is now growing noticeably stronger.

Some time ago, God gave me an analogy from the story of the children of Israel, regarding the "daring faith" that is necessary to truly 'take the promised land'. He showed me that the twelve spies who went in to spy out the promised land were really just like "prophets", who have been shown in the spirit what the Revival of tomorrow will be like - a land "flowing with milk and honey". However, in the end result, ONLY TWO of these spies (or prophets) - Joshua and Caleb - had the 'daring faith' necessary to "take the kingdom by force". The other ten spies, even though they had been shown what was to come, simply did not possess the spiritual "daring" necessary to take what God had promised. Even though they had truly been shown things by God, they preached an insipid, compromising word, and all who trusted in them perished in the wilderness. Joshua and Caleb, the "daring" prophets (and their families) were the only ones from that entire generation, who made it through into the promised land. The rest all fell at the final hurdle - the last great 'test'. Their prophets had let both them, and God, down very badly.

What this analogy illustrates is something which all history attests to be true. It is that mild, insipid, "reasonable" men can never lead God's people into true Reformation and Revival. What He really needs is daring, uncompromising "warriors" to lead His people at such times. Genuine moves of God have always been the most violent, the most controversial, the most revolutionary spiritual events of their day (and this applies even more to the "time of the end").

What God has shown me very clearly (and this applies to all ministries who hope to have a part in the coming great move of God) is that: It is not "who prophesies wins"; it is not even necessarily "who prays wins"; but rather, it is "WHO DARES WINS". This is the secret to becoming part of the new move of God. For He must have bold, 'daring' warriors to lead His people in such dark and deceptive times. "WHO DARES WINS" applies to every would-be Reformation/Revival ministry. It is simply only those who "dare" who will make it.

Sadly there is an old saying:- "The previous move persecutes the new move of God." And in the current scenario, we would have to say that the PROPHETIC/ APOSTOLIC MOVEMENT must surely now be regarded as the "previous" move (as well as whole sections of the Charismatic movement). But is it really possible that large elements of these movements might oppose or persecute the very 'new move' that they themselves have prophesied? Yes, it is possible. (It has happened before). We need to remember that envy and jealousy have been the hidden motives for much opposition to Revivals in the past, and this time will be no different.

THRIVING IN THE CRISIS

As has been intimated all the way through this book, the keys to surviving and even "thriving" in this present crisis are 'SPIRITUAL' in nature. The root causes of this crisis are spiritual and the answers are spiritual also. Those who merely prepare in physical or practical ways will find this out to their great cost. If you want to survive and even thrive, prepare yourself "spiritually" above all else. Spend time seeking God, get rid of all sin, obey Him implicitly, help the poor, leave behind the shallow "junk" of our culture and become a radical disciple of Jesus! If you have a family to care for, put the same principles into practice. Become a RADICAL FAMILY for Christ! Don't delay. We are out of time.

Such "spiritual" preparations are by far the most important answer to "surviving and thriving" in these dark times. But don't just selfishly seek God so you can "survive". Seek Him for His own sake. Become a true disciple who lives for Christ – not for what you can "get out of it" – but because your deepest desire is to utterly glorify Him.

The fact is, only those who have died to pride, died to shallowness and died to the desire to glorify themselves, can ever hope to have a part in the coming move of God. Truly, "many that are first shall be last, and many that are last shall be first." This Revival is to be born in a 'stable' rather than a palace – and those who will be involved in it will be a company of the humblest kind – tried, broken, trained and tested – who will emerge from the deserts as if from nowhere, full of the glory of God, hearts washed white as snow, with a mighty word in their mouths.

We live in the most momentous of days. May the Lamb who was slain truly receive the reward of His suffering.

Friend, are you prepared and ready to be a part of what He is about to do?

VISIT OUR WEBSITE –

http://www.revivalschool.com

Printed in the United States
127390LV00001B/24/P